# Loop -d-Loop

MORE THAN 40
NOVEL DESIGNS
FOR KNITTERS

# Loop -d-Loop

MORE THAN 40
NOVEL DESIGNS
FOR KNITTERS

## Teva Durham

PHOTOGRAPHS BY
ADRIAN BUCKMASTER

STC CRAFT | A MELANIE FALICK BOOK
NEW YORK

*To my parents, Minerva and David, and Jerry too,*
*for their example of creativity and hard work.*

**Edited by Melanie Falick**

**Book Design: Anna Christian**
**Production Director: Kim Tyner**

Published in 2005 by
STC Craft | A Melanie Falick Book
115 West 18th Street
New York, NY 10011
www.abramsbooks.com

Canadian Distribution:
Canadian Manda Group
One Atlantic Avenue, Suite 105
Toronto, Ontario M6K 3E7
Canada

Library of Congress Cataloging-in-Publication Data
Durham, Teva.
  Loop-d-loop / Teva Durham ; photographs by Adrian Buckmaster.
    p. cm.
  Includes bibliographical references and index.
  ISBN 1-58479-414-3 (alk. paper)
  1. Knitting—Patterns. 2. Knitwear. I. Title.

TT825.D77 2005
746.43'2041—dc22

2004017476

The text of this book was composed in Gotham and Tribute.

Printed in China

10 9 8 7 6 5 4 3 2 1
*First Printing*

Stewart, Tabori & Chang is a subsidiary of

LA MARTINIÈRE
GROUPE

# CONTENTS

# INTRODUCTION

SINCE YOU'RE LOOKING AT THIS BOOK, CHANCES ARE YOU'VE BECOME OBSESSED BY knitting, as I have. You may have recognized my name from designs or articles in knitting magazines, or you may have ordered kits or patterns from my website, loop-d-loop.com. In that case, you have an idea of what I'm about. But if you've come across the book by chance, you might wonder if "loop-d-loop" is some contraption or specific technique. It's not.

Loop-d-loop is my line of contemporary handknit designs, intended for boutique sale and knitting patterns. It's named for the process of knitting, which basically boils down to making a loop in another loop. I want my designs to reveal the craft at its most elemental and to focus on the experience of forming knit fabric. To do this, I often emphasize a single technique or tradition and blow it out of proportion (such as colossal bobbles or a massive cable) so the hand-wrought is "in your face."

The name also has a philosophical correlation for me—a loop-d-loop is a figure eight, a double helix, and thus it symbolizes infinity. I want my designs to express the deeper meaning I have found through knitting—therefore, I may use symbolic motifs or reference costume history with a hint of ecclesiastical or Elizabethan styling. I believe that with such dramatic and ceremonial elements, knits can explore visual metaphors just like museum-sanctioned art; I seek the subtext in this textile medium.

A loop-d-loop is also an aviator's feat, and I like to see myself as an aviatrix of knits, daring to break new boundaries. I try to infuse my designs with a sense of adventure and a bit of whimsy. I want to tap into what keeps us knitting—the suspense of watching the formation of fabric, the glee of following the twists and turns of the instructions, and the satisfaction of producing an object that is at once a replica of the sample and one's own unique rendition. Those are the challenges I give myself in designing the loop-d-loop line, all the while aiming for attractive knits with good fit.

This book presents eleven patterns from the original collection, updated with new yarn and/or sizes, plus more than thirty totally new projects created in the same spirit. The designs are grouped into three chapters, each of which features a "gallery" of images with commentary, then a section of instructions also with plenty of inspirational photos. The first chapter focuses on circular knits, the second on textural stitchwork, and the third on colorwork. By no means is this an all-encompassing tome of every possible type of knitting, but the designs cover a large range of knitting genres. I've tried to include ample technical information and tips for success but, to have space to present more designs, I haven't reproduced illustrations of knitting techniques. To supplement your own resources and knowledge, I suggest you invest in a good reference book for your at-home library, search online, join a knitting group, subscribe to knitting magazines, and frequent your local yarn shop. This book is geared to stir your creativity and help your knitting life take new flight. You can reproduce the items exactly or use the novel techniques and constructions as design inspiration.

I encourage the latter, because I believe we are all capable of genius. I have been amazed by naïve solutions of beginning students who come up with some quirky armhole or neck that nevertheless looks fresh from the runway. My approach to knit design is to know as many of the advanced techniques and "rules" as possible and then to strive to forget them, to break them, or to use them so the discipline appears effortless. Musicians and dancers, when they are great, do this. I consider knitting just as important an art form. Jazz music or modern dance may be universal languages that touch the soul, but isn't as well the urge to clothe the body with our own hands? And so I hope to elevate the respect shown for our "hobby" with my work. Everyone now says knitting is trendy and spiritual, but the items we're knitting need to speak for themselves.

❧

I've never been a linear, logical thinker, but possess what is joked at as female thought patterns. I skirt around issues, make analogies, and want to see from many perspectives—everything is relative. I have always searched for some means of expression to reveal the truths and ironies I see. I studied acting and then writing. My parents being painters, I always felt some practical profession would be a copout. While pursuing these careers (basically floundering as an eternal bohemian student), my knitting habit took over. At first I found in wordless, meaningless knitting a sanctuary from the pressure to perform or communicate. I discovered that a sweater (unlike a screenplay I procrastinated on) was something I could easily complete by building on it day by day. Then I realized that everything in my experience had prepared me for designing knits—from enthusiasm for crafts as a child to vintage-clothes collecting as a teenager. And once I got a foothold in knit design, I strived to make the kind of artistic statement I would want from any other medium.

With the aid of computers to nano-calculate, physicists are beginning to prove the universe is based on "organized chaos": a creative flow in which free will is self-determined but in constant improvisation with natural law, an idea also expressed in the teachings of Zen Buddhism and the I Ching.* It is also like

*I highly recommend Douglas Hofstadter's 1979 Pulitzer Prize–winning *Gödel, Escher, Bach: An Eternal Golden Braid*, which explores, in a chaotic dialogue, how patterns in math, art, and music reveal the essence of consciousness.

the knit design process—I am forming something that could have many variations, but takes shape through both choice and chance. I sketch my idea, drawing a kind of dressed-up paper doll. I begin each time with trepidation, an inkling of something to be created, but the ideas assert themselves on the blank page. The sketches peer out at me like imaginary friends, like sides of myself. I really enjoy this part, as it reminds me of being about seven years old. It has occurred to me that I have returned to what I loved at that age, as Michael Apted's documentary *Seven Up*—in which he chronicles the lives of seven-year-olds, then revisits them at seven-year increments to observe how seeds present at an early age flower later in life—posits we all will.

Swatching and choosing yarn can be a difficult process until I hit upon the exact combination. Then, as I tend to use a body-conscious silhouette, I work the pattern out using my dress form or an actual model's measurements. When a knitted piece is finished, I have a déjà vu sensation. Forgetting all the agony and hard work it took before the deadline, I feel it is as it was destined to be, as if it arrived fully formed. It's like the first time I saw my daughter. In labor, I couldn't believe a baby would emerge, it was so awesome an event. But there she was—the exact baby I would've dreamed up for myself if that's how babies were got. So over and over I experience a renewal of faith by designing and knitting, faith in both myself and the universe.

❧

I've assigned skill levels to each pattern: Easy, Easy Challenge, Intermediate, Intermediate Challenge, and Advanced. I urge you to take on challenges—instructions can be daunting, especially for the math phobic, but if you read the pattern once through for an overall understanding, try out any new technique, seek help if necessary, swatch for gauge, and then follow each pattern line character by character, it will all add up. Awareness is key—closely observe the movement of your needle tips, how the loops hang on the needle, and the structure and pattern of the emerging fabric to figure out what you're forming. Relax. Knitting is not rocket science or brain surgery. If you're motivated you can do what I did—teach yourself as many advanced techniques as possible and even invent new ones. Of course, sometimes even the most seasoned knitter just wants mindless stitching, so I offer that too.

Many experienced knitters act as if they have nothing more to learn in terms of their hand motions. But consider the years it takes to finesse a tennis serve or golf swing. If you find yourself in a rut, try knitting to a symphony, attempting to fall in line with the tempo of each movement. Or try knitting with the yarn held in the other hand or knitting back backward—just to shake yourself up a bit. Some new knitters feel they must achieve regulated, tight, mechanical-looking, even stitches. But that is a goal that takes practice, plus I think it is the wrong one—it makes fingers overly controlled and tense. The better challenge is to relax and strive for natural grace, fluidity of hand movement, and a gauge that is proportionate to the needle size. Let there be some rough-hewn, irregular areas—it is wonderful to see evidence that a fabric has been handknit. If knitting is a joyful experience and you have been "in the flow," it will resonate in the stitches. If you were frustrated and battling with the needles and yarn, it will also show. Think about your hands as extensions of your whole body. Quiet the movement down, but make sure the blood is flowing to the extremities and your breath is circling.

Finally, a word on yarn. I've included a variety here in terms of fiber, weight, and price. Please allow yourself the best materials you can afford. Yarn is like a living thing, a pet or plant that with care can give you years of companionship. While knitting, you are passing every inch of yarn through your hands, and it shows rough treatment. Clean hands, smooth nails, and smooth skin are actually very important. Sometimes a particular needle material fits better with certain yarn, reducing the chance of snagging or splitting. When you wind a ball from a hank, wind loosely so the fiber will not be stressed. And I believe in as little blocking as possible. In most cases, a nice shot of steam does wonders for natural fibers and allows you to mold the silhouette like a dressmaker, but stretching, pinning, using too much heat, or actual pressing can zap all the life out of yarn, rendering it like overprocessed hair. Sometimes it's best just to knit and wear a garment—there'll be more character, more depth to the cables, more ripple of stockinette against garter. Even the curl of an unribbed hem adds authenticity.

❧

I hope you enjoy these designs as much as I enjoyed creating them. In the introduction to each I've tried to convey my creative process and philosophy of knitting. This book truly reflects my vision—even the models are styled to replicate my imaginings of a magical realm, one in which everyone is clad in handknits.

*Teva*

# CHAPTER 1

# CYCLES

*Explorations in Circular Knitting:
Tubes, Spirals,
and Round Shapes*

PERHAPS YOU ARE LIKE MANY AVID KNITTERS: AS YOUR FINGERS MOVE steadily through the repetitive motions of working stitches, you experience a soothing, meditative state—you might even call it spiritual. Perhaps like me, you find this quality especially true of knitting circularly. With this technique, a favorite of famous knitters from the Virgin Mary (at least, as depicted in fourteenth-century images) to teacher and author Elizabeth Zimmermann, the rhythmic flow of knitting is never interrupted. There's no need to stop and turn your work at the end of a row, nor to purl for Stockinette stitch—a benefit for novices who may find purling awkward. Nor must the gratification of finishing a piece be delayed by seaming. Instead, there's the thrill of constructing as you go—the magic of seeing a three-dimensional object, like a sock, evolve. After all, much of our knitting is intended to fit around the human body.

For me, knitting in the round taps into the mysteries of the universe. People of many religions and cultures finger rings of prayer beads in spiritual devotion. Ceremonial circles are inherent in Native American pow-wows, Sufi whirling, and maypole dances. Circular movement connects us to the cyclical rhythms of existence: the orbit of planets, the days, the seasons, the very cycle of life. The circle represents motion itself, from the wheel, to ripples in water, to halos of light. Based on this geometry of nature we create meaning in the world, as evidenced by compasses, clocks, Stonehenge, Tibetan mandalas, Celtic crosses, and rose windows in Gothic cathedrals. Carl Jung discussed the circle as the symbol of the self, of the totality of the psyche. When Shakespeare's Hamlet wonders whether to "shuffle off this mortal *coil*," it connotes the globe, the wheel of fortune, life as a tangle of problems, thoughts as an obsessively repetitive cycle, and, literally, coil-like brain tissue. Leonardo DaVinci drew a man in a circle with limbs extended to meet the perimeter, to mark the navel as the center of the human compass. And that image of the Madonna knitting in the round is, to me, proof of everything my own journey into knitting has led me to believe: Circular knitting is a very old form, steeped in spirituality.

When I design, I'm often on a quest to connect the knitting experience to spiritual practice and the humanities, and that is most true of the designs in this chapter. The projects celebrate the circle, explore the tubular form of our bodies, and use circular needles in novel ways and, I hope, to delightful ends.

## knit choker collar and cuff

What could be simpler than a strip of fabric laced together to form a ring? And where better to place one than on neck and wrist? The desire to adorn these parts of the body transcends time, culture, and the dictates of fashion: My toddler puts her head or hand through any object with a hole to accommodate it and admires herself (yarn hanks and Starbucks cup protectors are her favorites). If you share this fascination, these knitted accoutrements may become yours. If anyone questions their function, reply that they cover your pulse points—spots of vulnerability and potential power.

Loop-d-loop designs often put dramatic focus on the neck—thanks, in part, to an exhibit at the Costume Institute of New York's Metropolitan Museum of Art, "Extreme Beauty," which inspired me to go with my instinct to do so. I peruse the exhibit's catalog frequently—it illustrates how various cultures have adorned the neck, from the dramatic beaded tire-sized rings of the Ndebele and platter-sized seventeenth-century ruffs to awesome collars from contemporary designers.

*>> See pattern on page 34.*

## chain link scarf

When teaching my circular knitting classes, I often illustrate how *not* to join a round by twisting a strip of paper before joining the ends. This demonstration reminds me of the construction-paper chains I made in kindergarten. I brought them home with a conflicted sense of accomplishment. My parents said the teacher stifled my creativity—she had punished me for coloring a pumpkin purple on a Thanksgiving banner. But my parents seemed somewhat unreliable, too; when I repeated their comments to my teacher, I got sent to the corner for "wisecracking." So I began to take solace in regimentation: a common task shared with other kids. One at a time, I looped strips and glued them, red and then green, into a Christmas garland.

These memories started me wondering if a chain could be knit. What would happen if you placed one tip of a circular needle through the center of a knit tube and *then* joined the round—would the needle or yarn get stuck, or would the yarn ball have to be constantly pulled through the center? I was surprised to find it worked without a hitch.

*>> See pattern on page 35 (scarf shown with, left to right, Irregular Rib Raglan with Toggle [page 90] and Slinky Tree Bark Rib Tunic [page 88]).*

## one-shoulder tunic

Often, the simplest shape is the most elegant. This top is basically a tube with a bit of shaping and a slit for one arm, lending a classical Greek look. The Greeks only wore sleeves in dramas; in daily life, they merely draped fabrics around their bodies and secured them with clasps. Their aesthetic was to perfect and reveal the body, and they exposed bare arms even when the Mediterranean climate turned cool (not an easy societal dictate for the old, infirm, and hormonally challenged).

Still, even as I sit knitting and munching pretzels, there is something in me (maybe in you, too) that yearns for this ideal: to attain the level of fitness at which you feel dressed even when almost naked. I'm often drawn to skimpy styles, thinking that if I buy them—or knit them—I'll strive to look good in them. And if my biceps aren't perfect, I'll simply knit a wrap to cover that pinch of softness that won't budge.

*>> See pattern on page 36.*

## bobble u-neck

Bobbles—though usually not so giant as the globes that border this vest—are traditional to Aran knitting. It makes sense that knitters whose specialty was crossing columns of stitches would think to lift stitches and shape them into a ball. Bobbles serve well as counterpoints to cables, but I'm not always satisfied by their traditional uses: They often result in too-busy patterns and slightly clown-ish sweaters.

One of my design strategies is to take a technique, isolate it, and blow it out of proportion. Bobbles taken to a sculptural extreme make this very basic chunky knit entertaining to make and wear. Like rolling balls of cookie dough or patting together meatballs, making these little bundles of stitches form rounded shapes satisfies some childlike urge.

>> See pattern on page 38.

## corkscrew scarf

While knitting a circle from the radius around with short rows (a common way to form a beret) I accidentally knit too many rows, so my work overlapped itself at the starting point. About to unravel my mistake, I held the swatch by a corner and—eureka! Knitting a narrow strip of short row wedges in the same direction, I correctly surmised, would create a spiral as curly as rotelli pasta. This concept became my guarded secret—such a simple recipe, really, that once it was out in the public domain, no one would need the instructions.

Isn't that the case with most secret recipes? The matriarch, in her last breath, passes on long-awaited wisdom: "Add olive oil after the water evaporates, then put the lid on" (actually, that's my Ecuadorian nanny's secret to perfect rice, my best attempt at letting you in on a family recipe). This project is one every yarn shop can suggest to customers who want to whip up something special with a ball or two of novelty yarn. I tried several different furry yarns before selecting this metallic. I appreciate the contrast between a hard-looking material—like burnished bronze—and soft styling. In a silver color, this scarf will truly reference the common corkscrew. Chin-chin!

>> See pattern on page 40.

## cowl with optional drawstring and trim

One day a decade ago, when I was a proofreader with a long commute, I wore a sheer blouse and light blazer to the office so I could leave straight from it for a fancy date. By lunch, the weather had turned for the worse, so I borrowed yarn and needles from my work in progress and, during my downtime, knit a loose turtleneck dickey based on the traditional Icelandic yoked (Lopi) sweater. It was the first prototype of my cowl. Later, after I had worked at *Vogue Knitting*, a friend asked me to design some handknits to complement the cut-and-sew shrugs he was selling to boutiques. I asked Trisha Malcolm, *VK*'s editor, if she wanted to publish the design. Thankfully, she advised me that I'd do better to retain the rights to this unique piece and sell the pattern on my own. Thus, loop-d-loop was launched, with a small ad in the back of *VK*. Variations are shown on pages 42–43.

>> See pattern on page 42 (Cowl shown with Corrugated Hat [page 84]).

## octagon purse

I have a love-hate relationship with handbags. I covet designer styles in shop windows and glossy ads—the shapes, detailing, and colors provoke the *Sex and the City* psyche that promises a new accessory will transform my life. But some status bags are downright tacky and cost as much as a car, while knockoffs can be had for twenty dollars from street vendors. And having spent my twenties as a vegan, I still have qualms about the commercialization of hide. That's why the recent prevalence of knit bags excites me. One of my favorite shapes is a rounded saddlebag that encircles the shoulder. I realized I could convert my cowl pattern into one of these bags by offsetting the center of the octagon (normally the neck) to form a handle. My first version, in felted mohair, appeared in the Summer 2003 issue of *Interweave Knits*. In that same issue, I did a pullover in "Safari," a linen-blend yarn that has a remarkable suedelike appearance perfect for accessories (and a great vegan alternative). Here, I've combined the two for a true knitter's status bag.

>> *See pattern on page 44.*

## café chair slipcovers

I was once foolish enough to buy a sunny yellow sofa even though Cooper, my border collie–lab mix, has never been known to forgo the comforts of home. In two months it looked like a spotty old banana. Its warranty did not include pet damage, and multiple cleaning products only spread the paw prints. Thus my first slipcover: I churned out yards and yards of fabric on my knitting machine and crocheted the pieces together to create folding lines along the contours of the couch. The slipcover was a success, resembling a modern Euro designer piece way out of my budget. Later, I thought about covering a folding chair in angora and using it to display my knits outside a storefront. Something diverted me from that plan, but I had great fun making these. You will, too.

>> *See pattern on page 46.*

## ballet t-shirt

Probably few people remember the moment they discovered the difference between knit and woven fabrics, but I do. One day in high school, I looked down at my green Adidas T-shirt, saw all the little V's of its fabric—just like a sweater—and *zap!* I realized that T-shirts are knit. I don't know why I had never made this connection before, having woven, knit, and sewed, but no matter—the T-shirt still fascinates me.

The T-shirt has a remarkable history; thanks to World Wars I and II, Marlon Brando in *A Streetcar Named Desire*, Jacqueline Bisset in *The Deep*, and *Miami Vice*, this men's under-garment has evolved into a unisex, sexy wardrobe staple (to read about it for yourself, check out www.vintageskivvys.com). Here is my take on the T-shirt: a stretchy, sheer, seamless, large-needle knit, worked with a continuous strand of yarn so you can put it on, undo the final stitch, and unravel it by spinning around, as one London performance artist did.

>> *See pattern on page 48.*

## yoke vest

Like some other loop-d-loop pieces, this vest (below and right) was originally developed for boutique production with these criteria in mind: It must be obviously hand-knit with prominent full-fashioning marks, be quick to knit by hand but a pain to do on a factory machine, look modern yet nod to fashion history, be rustic yet clean in styling, and emphasize the lines of the female form. The shaping in the front and back of the bodice, an exercise in aligning paired decreases and increases, creates a directional hourglass in the fabric. It is reminiscent of the triangular corseted bodice worn above a farthingale, the bell-shaped hoopskirt of the Elizabethan era. I can also imagine this vest in a space-age color for a techno, sci-fi look.

>> See pattern on page 50.

## ruffled gloves

There's something ironic and tender about forming a knitted hand with your hands. While knitting this, as the little tubes for each digit emerged, I slipped my hand into the glove-in-progress to measure and sometimes just admire the seemingly complex shape that was evolving.

I couldn't decide on the cuff length for these gloves, so I made an asymmetrical pair. If you want to make opera-length gloves (which reach past the elbow) add a few inches' worth of stitches to the cast-on edge, then decrease gradually to the wrist. I used the same yarn as for the Felted Tweed Hat (page 54) so you can coordinate your accessories. You can adapt this pattern to make a tubular scarf by casting on for a tube 12 to 14 inches wide and working ruffles at each end.

>> See pattern on page 52.

## felted tweed hat

The process of making this hat was an exercise in accepting transformation. The yarn itself is complex, plied of two colors that are alternately obscured and revealed by knitting. I first swatched it in orangish red, then dark green, then bright green. I ruled out the red, felt the first green too somber, and thought the other too childish. So I cast on the hat with a strand of each green, and they combined into a tweedy blend with just enough depth, just enough tang. The moss stitch really suited the mossy color, and I loved how it looked without felting.

After I threw the hat in the washer, the textured pattern melded together, and long gray fibers emerged. The distinction between colors and stitch patterns dissolved into a grassy pelt. For embellishment, I chose a gray velvet ribbon, but it didn't fit the hat's character until I obscured it with embroidery, which showcased the beauty of the yarn right off the ball. Then I used my swatches to create a flower. The result is a hat with a life of its own, something more than the sum of its knitted parts.

*>> See pattern on page 54 (hat shown with Unisex Basketweave V-neck [page 100]).*

## puff sleeve bolero

As the shrug reaches its fashion denouement, it's no surprise that attempts to reinvent it abound. While window-shopping in trendy NoLita (North of Little Italy in New York City), I spotted several bolero or "Spencer" jackets—basically shrugs with a bit more fabric. I decided to reinterpret a fetching one with puffy sleeves as a handknit. I had an advantage over the patternmaker of the tailored version: I was creating the fabric myself, so shaping the pouf could be done many ways and wherever I liked—by working increases, by adding another strand of yarn and changing needle size to alter the weight of the fabric, or by using ribbing to draw in the flat pieces and curve them into rounded shapes. I like to think outside of the cut-and-sew model and explore instead the possibilities inherent in shaping knitting, so I put all of these techniques into this abbreviated garment.

*>> See pattern on page 56.*

## "cast-away" fringe pullover

Raglan yoke sweaters knit in the round are my most frequent construction, perhaps because they are so basic. I return to them over and over to try variations. Here, I wanted the garment itself to be solidly circular, but the edges to be deconstructed. I wanted a shredded, washed-up-on-the-shore-of-a-desert-island effect. I didn't want to apply fringe during the finishing, and I didn't want fringe per se, but rather a shorn, frayed edge, so I experimented with knitted-in fringe. I came up with this process of casting on and binding off, which allows a gradual hemline. The fringe created was curlier than I anticipated, but I decided to emphasize this quality with a thick-and-thin hand-dyed yarn. The result: dreadlocks, like the fleece of a wild, wayward sheep.

>> See pattern on page 58.

## dreamcatcher medallion cardigan

When I set out to develop a sweater with a medallion for this book, I first looked to Norah Gaughan's Sunburst Pullover design, which I greatly admire. In it, the front and the back begin as circular medallions knit out from the center; a traditional raglan shape is then constructed around them. I planned to do likewise and started to make the calculations, then I spoke to Norah, who said she wished she had done the reverse: left space for the medallion, then filled it in. In my version, this approach was not only easier, as Norah had fore-seen, but it allowed me to assemble the entire sweater and try it on before deciding how to fill in the circle.

Opting for a spiderweb look, I knit the medallion inward with a lacy dropped garter stitch. But when I bound it off, a hole still formed in the center. I considered decreasing to fewer stitches or drawing the stitches together to close it, then I realized what I had created: not a spiderweb, but a dreamcatcher. The Lakota believe that the dreamcatcher, a webbed willow hoop adorned with feathers and beads, was given by Iktomi (a trickster spider) to be placed above the bed, where good forces would be caught in the web and bad forces sifted out through the center hole. Other Native Americans borrow this tradition, but most believe the opposite—that the web will retain bad energy so only good energy will fall through the hole to the sleeper.

>> See pattern on page 60.

# knit choker collar and cuff

## collar

Using smaller needles, 1 strand of yarn, and long-tail cast-on method, cast on 47 sts. Work 5 rows in 1x1 Rib, working simple eyelet buttonholes at each edge on Row 3 as foll:

**Row 1:** (WS) * P1, k1; rep from * to last st, p1.

**Row 2:** * K1, p1; rep from * to last st, k1.

**Row 3:** Eyelet Buttonhole Row—P1, yo, p2tog; work as established to last 3 sts; p2tog, yo, p1.

**Row 4:** * K1, p1; rep from * to last st, k1.

**Row 5:** * P1, k1; rep from * to last st, p1.

Change to larger needles and St st (knit on RS, purl on WS); join a second strand of yarn (2 strands now held together).

**Row 6:** (RS) Knit.

**Rows 7–9:** Work even in St st.

Bind off all sts.

### FINISHING

Insert each end of cording from back to front through eyelet buttonholes at each edge of piece, tie, and make a knot at each end.

## cuff

Using smaller needles, 1 strand of yarn, and long-tail cast-on method, cast on 27 sts. Beg 1x1 Rib as follows:

**Row 1:** (WS) * P1, k1; rep from * to last st, p1.

**Row 2:** * K1, p1; rep from * to last st, k1.

Rep Rows 1 and 2 for 1x1 Rib.

Work even as established until piece measures 5" from beg; bind off all sts loosely in Rib.

### FINISHING

Weave in ends. Fold piece lengthwise to form a tube and lace up as you wish, then tie ends tog and make a knot at each end.

---

### KNITTED MEASUREMENTS

**Collar:** 2½" tall; 13½" around neck ribbing and 17" at lower edge

**Cuff:** 8" wide x 5" tall

### YARN

Karabella "Soft Tweed" (100% merino wool), worsted tweed, 2-ply with binder

1 ball (1.75oz/50g; 108yd/100m) in 1100 red (makes 1 collar and 1 cuff)

### NEEDLES/TOOLS

US 7 (4.5mm), or size to match gauge

US 13 (9mm), or size to match gauge (for collar only)

### NOTIONS

⅓ yd black leather, braided wool, or ultrasuede cording for collar

⅔ yd black leather, braided wool, or ultrasuede cording for cuff

### GAUGE

11 sts and 12 rows = 4" in St st using larger needles and 2 strands held together

14 sts and 24 rows = 4" in 1x1 Rib using smaller needles and 1 strand

Always check and MATCH gauge for best fit.

# chain link scarf

## OVERVIEW

For alternating scarf, make 1 teal link then 1 brown link; for the half and half scarf, make 10 links in purple at one side and 10 links in pink at the other side.

For a smoother top edge, after cutting the yarn and pulling it through the final st of the bind off, run it through the first bound off st of rnd to complete the st. Use the cast-on tail to clean up the lower edge in the same way.

## FIRST LINK

Using color of choice and long-tail cast-on method, cast on 32 sts. Pm on RH needle for beg of rnd. Join, being careful not to twist sts (see page 171).

Beg St st (knit every rnd); work even until piece measures 3" (about 11 rnds), from the cast-on edge. Bind off all sts loosely.

Weave in ends on WS.

## REMAINING LINKS

Using color of choice, cast on as for first Link.

**Attach Links together:** Insert the LH needle tip (the one without the yarn) through the center of the Link just completed. Pm on RH needle for beg of rnd. Join, being careful not to twist sts. (The yarn is to the back and above the needle and Links, so there will be no problem working rnds while linked through the other piece.)

Begin St st; work even until piece measures 3" (about 11 rnds) from the beg. Bind off all sts loosely.

Cont to add links in this manner (Links may be added to either end), until scarf measures approximately 6 feet (20 links), or desired length.

## KNITTED MEASUREMENTS

Each link is 3" tall with a 10½" circumference

**Scarves shown are 6 feet long with 20 links**

## YARN

Classic Elite Yarns "La Gran" (76.5% mohair/17.5% wool/6% nylon), brushed mohair, heavy worsted

2 balls each (1.5oz/42g; 90yd/82m) in 6518 teal and 6545 brown for alternating scarf

2 balls each in 6560 purple and 6599 pink for half and half scarf

## NEEDLES/TOOLS

US 10 ½ (6.5mm) 12" long circular, or size to match gauge

Stitch markers

*Note: If you find it awkward working with this shorter length circular needle, use one circular needle, any length, to hold the sts and a second one to knit around.*

## GAUGE

12 sts and 16 rnds = 4" in St st

Always check and MATCH gauge for best fit.

# one-shoulder tunic

## OVERVIEW

This tunic is knit in-the-round from neck down, in one piece. The one armhole is worked by binding off and casting on sts. Be aware that your cast on and bind off tension will greatly affect stretch/size of the opening; each cast on or bound off edge st should exactly equal the width of each column of sts on the garment below it, so that edge doesn't pucker—use a larger needle, if necessary, when casting on and binding off.

If you prefer not to have the natural roll on the edges—which is part of the design—finish the edges with a row of single crochet, or work 2 rows of 1x1 Rib at neck and hem.

There are no seams where yarn ends can be woven in; begin new balls at side where they will be less conspicuous.

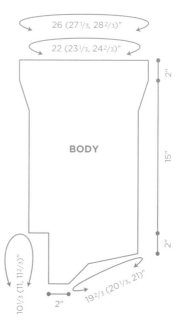

### SIZES

Small (Medium, Large)

*Note that fabric is very stretchy when choosing size.*

**Shown in size Small.**

### KNITTED MEASUREMENTS

**Chest:** 22 (23 1/3, 24 2/3)"

**Length to underarm:** 17"

### YARN

Trendsetter "Dolcino" (75% acrylic/25% polyamide), bulky woven ribbon

3 (4, 5) balls (1.75 oz/50g; 99yds/90m) in 32 slate blue

### NEEDLES/TOOLS

US 13 (9mm) 24" long circular, or size to match gauge

Stitch markers

### GAUGE

12 sts and 18 rnds = 4" in St st

Always check and MATCH gauge for best fit.

## NECK/SHOULDER STRAP/ CHEST

Using long-tail cast-on method, cast on 59 (61, 63) sts. Pm on RH needle for beg of round. Join, being careful not to twist sts (see page 171). Slipping marker every rnd, beg St st (knit every rnd); work even for 2 rnds.

**Begin Shaping:** Inc 1 st (k-f/b), at Front raglan and Back raglan of one shoulder every rnd as foll:

**Rnd 3:** K1, inc, k11, inc, knit to end of rnd.

**Rnd 4:** K1, inc, k13, inc, knit to end of rnd.

**Rnds 5-8:** Cont as established, working 2 more sts between incs every rnd—71 (73, 75) sts.

**Rnd 9:** K6, bind off 17 sts, knit to end of rnd.

**Rnd 10:** Shape Underarm—K6, cast on 12 (14, 16) sts using single cast-on method, (fold yarn into loop around thumb and place on RH needle so that yarn end is to inside, pull to tighten, but be aware of your tension), knit to end of rnd—66 (70, 74) sts.

## TORSO

Cont in St st, work even until piece measures 12" from underarm.

**Next Rnd:** K11 (12, 13) (there should be 1 st before side "seam," centered under the cast on sts for underarm), inc, pm, inc, k31 (33, 35), inc, pm (other side "seam"), inc, knit to end —70 (74, 78) sts.

Work 3 rnds even.

* **Next Rnd:** Inc 1 st before and after each marker—74 (78, 82) sts.

Work 3 rnds even.

Rep from * once—78 (82, 86) sts.

**Divide for Side Slit:** Beg working back and forth in rows; work Front and Back separately from seam to seam as foll:

**Front:** Knit across to marker, turn (WS of fabric facing). Purl to marker at beg of rnd; leave yarn hanging ready for RS row.

**Back:** With WS facing, join a new ball of yarn to next st; purl across to marker, turn; knit to marker at beg of rnd where other ball waits for RS row; leave yarn hanging ready for WS row.

Cont in St st (knit on RS, purl on WS), work 2 rows on Front alternately with 2 rows on Back as established until piece measures 2" from beg of side slits. Bind off all sts loosely.

Weave in ends.

*Hint: With this slinky ribbon yarn it's best to tie ends securely onto a purl loop on the wrong side of fabric and to cut short.*

# bobble u-neck

## OVERVIEW

Garment is knit in one piece in-the-round from hem to underarm, and then Front and Back are worked separately in rows to shoulder. To make bobbles more easily on this large needle, be sure to wrap yarn around fullest part of needle rather than on the narrower tip and insert needle tip into st to its full girth each time. Otherwise, it may be difficult to work 5 times into the same st—or the initial 5 loops of the bobble will be tight and difficult to manipulate. This will cause the bobble not to be as full and round as desired.

## SPECIAL TECHNIQUE

**Make bobble [mb]:** Knit into front, back, front, back, front of next st, turn; p5, turn; k2tog, k1, k2tog, turn; p3tog; turn to RS and place rem st on RH needle.

## BODY

Cast on 60 (66, 72) sts. Pm on RH needle for beg of rnd. Join, being careful not to twist sts (see page 171).

**Rnd 1:** P1, * mb, p2; rep from * to last st, p1—20 (22, 24) bobbles made.

Cont in Rev St st (purl every rnd), work even for 7 rnds.

**Rnd 9:** Shape Sides—P2tog, p26 (29, 32), p2tog, pm for side seam; p2tog, p26 (29, 32), p2tog—56 (62, 68) sts.

Work even for 2 rnds.

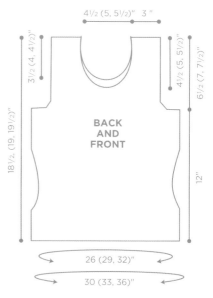

## SIZES

Small/Medium (Medium/Large, X-large)
*Note that fabric is very stretchy when choosing size.*

**Shown in size Small/Medium.**

## KNITTED MEASUREMENTS

Chest: 30 (33, 36)"
Waist: 26 (29, 32)"
Length: 18½ (19, 19½)" total

## YARN

Tahki "Baby" (100% merino), bulky 2-ply

4 (5, 5) balls (3.5oz/100g; 60yd/55m) in 35 burnt orange

## NEEDLES/TOOLS

US 17 (12mm) 24" long circular, or size to match gauge

Stitch markers

Stitch holders

## GAUGE

8 sts and 10 rnds/rows = 4" in Rev St st

Always check and MATCH gauge for best fit.

**Rnd 12:** * P2tog, purl to 2 sts before marker, p2tog; rep from * to end—52 (58, 64) sts.

Work even for 2 rnds.

**Rnd 15:** * Inc (p-f/b), purl to 1 st before marker, inc; rep from * to end—56 (62, 68) sts.

Work even for 5 rnds.

**Rnd 21:** * Inc, purl to 1 st before marker, inc; rep from * to end—60 (66, 72) sts.

Work even until piece measures 12" from cast on edge.

**Divide for Armholes:** Bind off 3 sts, purl across to side marker, turn. (WS) Bind off 3 sts, k24 (27, 30) (you are now at the first bind off, having worked across the sts for the Back); turn. Place rem sts on holder (leave on other side of circular needle or put on spare needle) for Front.

**BACK**
**Row 1:** (RS) Shape armhole—K1, p2tog, purl to last 3 sts, p2tog, k1—22 (25, 28) sts.

**Row 2:** Knit.

**Row 3:** K1, mb, purl to last 2 sts, mb, k1.

Cont as established, knit first and last st of RS rows for selvedge, work even for 3 rows.

**Row 7:** K1, mb, p4 (6, 7), mb (at neck edge), p3;

**Sizes Small/Medium and X-large only:** Make a bobble while knitting tog next 2 sts to dec 1 st and center the bobble at neck edge: Insert RH needle from front to back through next 2 sts as if to k2tog, treat them as 1 st, make bobble as before;

**Size Medium/Large only:** Make bobble;

**All sizes:** P3, mb (at neck edge), p4 (6, 7), mb, k1—21 (25, 27) sts.

**Row 8:** (WS) K6 (8, 9), bind off center 9 sts, k6 (8, 9), turn.

Working each side separately, shape straps and neck as foll:

**BACK RIGHT SHOULDER STRAP AND NECK**
**Row 1:** (RS) K1, p4; p2tog 0 (1, 1) time, k1—6 (7, 8) sts.

**Row 2:** Knit.

**Row 3:** K1, mb (at armhole edge), p2 (3, 4), mb (at neck edge), k1.

**Row 4:** Knit.

**Row 5:** K1, p4 (3, 4), p2tog 0 (1, 1) time, k1—6 (6, 7) sts.

**Row 6:** Knit.

**Row 7:** (RS) K1, mb (at armhole edge), p2 (2, 3), mb (at neck edge), k1.

Maintaining 1 st each side as selvedge st, work even in Rev St st for 3 (4, 3) rows.

**Size Small/Medium and Large only:** Bind off rem sts.

**Size X-large only: Row 11:** K1, mb (at armhole edge), p3, mb (at neck edge), k1.

**Row 12:** Knit.

Bind off rem sts.

**BACK LEFT SHOULDER STRAP AND NECK**
(RS) Join yarn at left neck edge; work as for Right Strap and Neck, reversing shaping.

**FRONT**
With RS facing, join yarn at Left armhole. Cont in Rev St st, bind off 3 sts at beg of next 2 rows—24 (27, 30) sts.

**Row 1:** (RS) Shape armhole—K1, p2tog, purl to last 3 sts, p2tog, k1—22 (25, 28) sts.

**Row 2:** Knit.

**Row 3:** K1, mb, purl to last 2 sts, mb, k1.

Cont as established, knit first and last st of RS rows for selvedge; work even for 1 row.

**Row 5:** K1, p6 (8, 9), mb (at neck edge), p2;

**Size Small/Medium and X-large only:** Make bobble in next 2 sts to dec 1 st as for Back;

**Size Medium/Large:** Make bobble;

**All sizes:** P2, mb (at neck edge), p6 (8, 9), k1—21 (25, 27) sts.

**Row 6:** (WS) K7 (9, 10), bind off center 7 sts for neck, k7 (9, 10).

Working each side separately, shape straps and neck as foll:

**FRONT LEFT STRAP AND NECK**
**Row 1:** (RS) K1, mb (at armhole edge), purl across to last 1 (3, 3) sts, p2tog 0 (1, 1) time, k1—7 (8, 9) sts.

**Row 2:** K1, ssk, knit to end—6 (7, 8) sts.

**Row 3:** K1, p3 (4, 5), mb (at neck edge), k1.

**Row 4:** K1, ssk 0 (1, 1) time, knit to end—6 (6, 7) sts.

**Row 5:** K1, mb (at armhole edge), p3 (3, 4), k1.

**Row 6:** Knit.

**Row 7:** K1, p3 (3, 4), mb (at neck edge), k1.

**Row 8:** Knit.

**Row 9:** K1, mb (at armhole edge), p3 (3, 4), k1.

Work even for 0 (1, 2) rows.

Bind off rem sts.

**FRONT RIGHT STRAP AND NECK**
(RS) Join yarn at right neck edge; work as for Left Strap and Neck, reversing shaping.

**FINISHING**
Join shoulder seams.

# corkscrew scarf

## OVERVIEW

You will be working a sequence of Short Rows to create wedgelike segments, each roughly a 60-degree triangle (see illustration), that build into a counterclockwise circle. The circle curls into a spiral when more than 6 wedges are completed and it grows beyond 360 degrees. In order to orient yourself for the direction of the short rows, place a marker at the left end of RS row and retie or rehang marker as necessary. Except for every 17th and 18th Row, you will always turn before reaching the end of the RS rows where the marker is attached; thus that edge will grow very slowly and become the inner vortex of the spiral. If you mistakenly work a wedge in the opposite direction, it adds length to the vortex, compensates for the previous wedge, and creates a flat area. Be sure to work a RS, then a WS row on all sts between each sequence of Short Rows. If you only work 1 row, then you'll start the sequence on the opposite side.

On the other hand, if you want to make an interesting flat scarf, you can alternate the direction of the short rows each segment by working only 1 row on all sts between each sequence.

## SPECIAL TECHNIQUE
**Short Row Shaping** (see page 171)

### KNITTED MEASUREMENTS
Scarf shown is 32" long (the inner/shorter edge dictates length)

### YARN
Berroco "Quest" (100% nylon), bulky tubular chain

2 hanks (1.75oz/50g; 82yd/76m) in 9813 rose glow (copper)

### NEEDLES/TOOLS
US 10 (6mm), or size to match gauge

(Shorter needle is more manageable for this narrow piece.)

Stitch marker

### GAUGE
12 sts and 24 rows = 4" in Garter st

*Note: Each Garter ridge = 2 rows when measuring gauge.*

Always check and MATCH gauge for best fit.

Cast on 10 sts.

* Row 1: (WS) K10.

Short Row 1: K8, wrp-t, k8.

Short Row 2: K7, wrp-t, k7.

Short Row 3: K6, wrp-t, k6.

Short Row 4: K5, wrp-t, k5.

Short Row 5: K4, wrp-t, k4.

Short Row 6: K3, wrp-t, k3.

Short Row 7: K2, wrp-t, k2.

Short Row 8: K1, wrp-t, k1.

Next Row: (RS) Knit across—10 sts.

*Note: Usually when working Short Rows, the wrap would be knit together with the st that it wraps.*

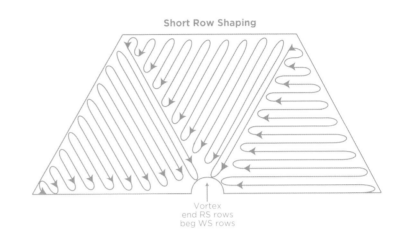

**Short Row Shaping**

Vortex
end RS rows
beg WS rows

*It is unnecessary here, as the Garter st and the texture of the yarn make it hard to see the wraps, but it may be done if desired.*

Rep from * for rem wedges.

When piece measures 32" long or desired length, bind off at the end of the Short Row sequence.

# cowl with optional drawstring and trim

**SIZES**

One size fits adult as cowl, child as capelet, toddler as poncho

**KNITTED MEASUREMENTS**

12" tall from hem to top

42" circumference at hem, 16" around neck

**YARN**

Brown Sheep "Naturespun" (100% wool) 3-ply worsted, (use double strand)

1 ball (3.5oz/100g; 245yd/224m) in 98 pink please (MC)
—OR—
1 ball in 522 nervous green (MC)
—OR—

Jaeger "Cashair" (65% cashmere/35% merino), super bulky tubular chain (use single strand)

3 balls (.875oz/25g; 51yd/47m) in 77 beaver (brown) (MC)

**OPTIONAL FURRY TRIM**

Jaeger "Fur" (47% kid mohair/47% wool/6% polyamid) super bulky (use single strand)

1 ball (1.75oz/50g; 22yd/20m) in 50 bear (brown) for pink cowl (CC)
—OR—
1 ball in 49 antelope (gray) for brown cowl (CC)

**OPTIONAL DRAWSTRING**

1 yd lacing or ribbon ¼"–¾" wide

**NEEDLES/TOOLS**

US 15 (10mm) 24" long circular, or size to match gauge

16 stitch markers

**GAUGE**

10 sts and 14 rnds =4" in St st, using 2 strands of Naturespun held together OR single strand of Cashair

Always check and MATCH gauge for best fit.

## OVERVIEW

This project is knit in the rnd from the bottom up in an octagon shape. After the hem, you begin with eight wedgelike segments of 12 sts each, with one st between each segment—like spokes of a wheel. The sides of each segment are shaped with mirrored decreases every fourth rnd until 4 sts remain in each segment. The remaining sts are then worked even for the neck.

Placing a marker (pm) at each side of the "spokes" helps to keep track of the decreases so that they will align vertically—slip markers (sl m) every rnd.

Each decrease (dec) is made up of 2 sts; when a segment has 12 sts, it allows for a dec (2 sts), 8 knits and another dec (2 sts), and will be reduced to a 10-st segment by the Decrease Rnd.

Use mirrored decreases—on the RH edge of each segment use a right-slanting dec and on the LH edge of each segment a left-slanting dec. The angled marks created by decreasing will point toward the spokes, rather than toward the center of each wedge, for a more decorative effect.

Use the decreases you are familiar with, or see page 171.

*Note: Instructions for optional Furry Trim, on lower edge and neck, are shown in < > where they differ from main piece.*

## COWL

Using long-tail cast-on method and <single strand of CC> or MC and appropriate number of strands for the yarn being used, loosely cast on 104 sts. Pm on RH needle for beg of rnd. Join, being careful not to twist sts (see page 171).

<Purl 1 rnd. Change to MC.>

Beg St st, using MC.

**Rnds 1–6:** Knit.

**Rnd 7:** Decrease Rnd—[K1, pm, right-slanting dec, k8, left-slanting dec, pm] 8 times—88 sts.

Work even for 3 rnds.

**\* Rnd 11:** Decrease Rnd—[K1, sl m, right-slanting dec, k6, left-slanting dec, sl m] 8 times—72 sts.

Work even for 3 rnds.

Rep from \* twice, working 2 less sts between mirrored decs each Decrease Rnd—40 sts.

## NECK

If not working casing for optional drawstring, skip Rnds 23 and 24.

**Rnd 23:** Eyelet Rnd—[K1, yo, left-slanting dec, left-slanting dec, yo] 8 times—40 sts. *Note: The yo's are incs and so compensate for the decs.*

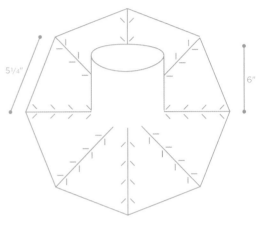

**Rnd 24:** Knit, treating each yo as a stitch.

Work even until neck measures 6" <5½">.

<Cut MC, join CC; knit 1 rnd, purl 1 rnd.> Bind off all sts—loosely! Be sure it will fit over wearer's head before cutting yarn. Block lightly.

# octagon purse

**KNITTED MEASUREMENTS**
13″ diameter x 2½″ deep

**YARN**
GGH/Muench "Safari" (78% linen/22% nylon), fiber-wrapped core, sport weight (use 4 strands held together)

4 spools (1.75oz/50g; 151yd/140m) in 27 nutmeg

**NEEDLES/TOOLS**
US 11 (8mm) 16″ long and 24″ long circular, or size to match gauge
Tapestry needle

**NOTIONS**
Lining: ½ yard stretch twill or other fabric, tailor's chalk, matching thread, scissors, sewing needle

**GAUGE**
12 sts and 16 rnds (rows) = 4″ in Rev St st with 4 strands held together
Always check and MATCH gauge for best results.

**OVERVIEW**

Knit from the center of the handle out, there are 8 segments of Reverse Stockinette st divided by Stockinette st spokes. You begin working in counterclockwise rnds (as normal), then work Short Rows (each composed of a RS row and a WS row), back and forth in a path that swings like a pendulum, the distance from one side to the other getting smaller as if the pendulum were slowing down. RS rows go counterclockwise (from right to left); WS rows go clockwise. You will be working M1 eyelet incs on either side of the spokes every other row. The wedge-like segments become bigger toward the bottom because those segments skipped over by the path of the short rows get fewer incs.

**SPECIAL TECHNIQUE**
**Short Row Shaping** (see page 171)

**SPECIAL TERM**
**M1 [open]—Eyelet inc:** Insert LH needle from front to back under strand of yarn between the st just worked and the next st; knit strand from LH needle through the front loop, inc 1 st and forming an eyelet.

**FRONT AND BACK**
(Both alike)

Using shorter needle and long-tail cast-on method, cast on 40 sts. Pm on RH needle for beg of rnd. Join, being careful not to twist sts—with the bumpy side facing, and yarn on RH needle, fold needle and pm for beg of rnd, purl into first st on LH needle to join.

**Rnd 1:** P4 (including joining st), k1, * p4, k1; rep from * across—8 St st spokes dividing 8 Rev St st segments; the last st is the top left spoke of purse between segments H and A (see diagram).

For remainder of piece, knit the knit sts and purl the purl sts as they face you; work all inc sts as purl on RS, knit on WS. When incs make shorter needle crowded, change to longer needle.

Work Short Row shaping as foll:

**Short Row 1:** [P4, M1 (see above), k1,

M1] 6 times, p2. You are in segment B; there are 8 sts rem in rnd; wrp-t; work as established until 2 sts before beg of rnd in segment H, wrp-t.

Short Row 2: [Work to spoke, M1, k1, M1] 5 times, purl to 2 sts before next spoke between segments B and C, wrp-t; work to 2 sts before spoke between segments G and H, wrp-t.

Short Row 3: [Work to spoke, M1, k1, M1] 4 times, purl to 2 sts before the last wrap in segment C, wrp-t; work to 2 sts before last wrap in segment G, wrp-t.

Short Row 4: [Work to spoke, M1, k1, M1] 4 times, purl to 2 sts before the last wrap in segment C, wrp-t; work to 2 sts before last wrap in segment G, wrp-t.

Short Row 5: [Work to spoke, M1, k1, M1] 3 times, purl to 3 sts before spoke between segments D and C, wrp-t; work to 3 sts before spoke between segments F and G, wrp-t.

Short Row 6: [Work to spoke, M1, k1, M1] 2 times, purl to 3 sts before the last wrap in segment D, wrp-t; work to 3 sts before last wrap in segment F, wrp-t.

Short Row 7: [Work to spoke, M1, k1, M1] 2 times, purl to 3 sts before the last wrap in segment D, wrp-t; work to 3 sts before last wrap in segment F, wrp-t.

Short Row 8: [Work to spoke, M1, k1, M1] 2 times, purl to 3 sts before the last wrap in segment D, wrp-t; work to 3 sts before last wrap in segment F, wrp-t.

Short Row 9: [Work to spoke, M1, k1, M1] 1 time, purl to 4 sts before spoke between segments E and D, wrp-t; work to 4 sts before spoke between segments E and F, wrp-t.

Short Row 10: Work to 4 sts before last wrap, wrp-t; work to 4 sts before last wrap, wrp-t.

Next Row: [Work to spoke, M1, k1, M1] 5 times, work to marker for beg of rnd.

Work even for 1 rnd.

Next Rnd: [Work to spoke, M1, k1, M1] 8 times—124 sts.

Work even for 2 rnds. Bind off all sts loosely purlwise.

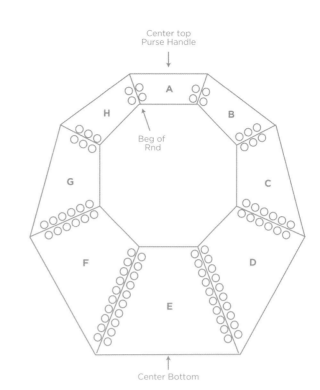

Center top Purse Handle

Beg of Rnd

Center Bottom

## GUSSET
(Work on Front only)

With WS facing, beg 5 sts from the spoke dividing segments B and C (see diagram), working into the sts of last row under the front and back loops of bound off edge, pick up and knit 85 sts around to 5 sts before the spoke dividing segments G and H. Work Short Row shaping in Rev St st as foll:

Short Row 1: (RS) Purl all sts, wrp-t; (WS) knit to 8 sts from end, wrp-t.

Short Row 2: Purl to 8 sts from end, wrp-t; knit to 10 sts before last wrapped st, wrp-t.

Short Row 3: Purl to 10 sts before last wrapped st, wrp-t; knit to 12 sts from last wrapped st, wrp-t.

Short Row 4: Purl to 12 sts from last wrapped st, wrp-t; knit to end, turn.

Bind off all sts purlwise, working wrapped sts together with their wraps as you come to them.

## FINISHING
Lining: To give the knit purse more form and prevent objects from poking out between sts, you can easily line it as I did. If you aren't using stretch fabric, cut lining pieces on the bias to better match the knit fabric's flexibility. Place fabric on table, folded along length, aligned with straight edge so that the fabric grain is straight. Lay Back (unattached side) of purse on fabric at a 45-degree angle using center spoke as guide. Outline with tailor's chalk—this will give you 2 pieces. Hold Front with bottom Gusset points at 45-degree angle to grain of fabric, outline open side of Gusset, then bend in purse to outline the attached side (not symmetrical). Cut out lining pieces, leaving ⅝″ seam allowance. With RS's facing, sew side Gusset piece of lining to Front and Back pieces of lining.

With 3 strands of yarn and tapestry needle, sew Back panel to Gusset, working under the front and back loops of bound off edge.

With WS's together, place lining into purse and fold under seam allowance, pin in place; using 1 strand of yarn and tapestry needle, whipstitch lining to inside edge of purse—cut seam allowance to ¼″ and tuck under as you go to ease fabric around curves.

# café chair slipcovers

## OVERVIEW

Chair cover is worked in-the-round; Corners (False Seams) are created by Drop/Latch Technique; they continue up from the lower section (the section that will cover the legs of the chair), along top edge of Seat and Backrest. The Seat is formed with a series of Short Rows, similar to the technique used for turning the heel of a sock or the instep of a baby bootie. However, pay close attention to the instructions; the ratio of dec is done for correct Seat length/width—EOR would be too long (38 rows); every row too short—so basically you will skip every 3rd opportunity to dec as given below.

## SPECIAL TECHNIQUE

**Drop/Latch False Seams:** (This will form the 4 corners at lower edge and continue along arms of slipcover.) Drop the st indicated in instructions off the needle, unravel down to cast on edge or last latched st; using crochet hook, pick up last loop; reform the column of sts (latch-up sts) 2 at a time by hooking 2 strands of ladder and pull through to form a large st; place last double st on needle and work as usual on following rnds.

## LOWER (LEG) SECTION

Cast on 124 sts. Pm on RH needle for beg of rnd (which is at RH side if facing Back of chair). Join, being careful not to twist sts (see page 171). Beg St st (knit every rnd).

Rnd 1: K30 for Back, pm; k32 for Left Side, pm; k30 for Front, pm; k32 for Right Side.

Rnds 2-9: Work even in St st, slipping markers (sl m).

Rnd 10: Decrease Rnd/Beg False Seams—* Drop/Latch first st, k28,

## SIZE

**To fit standard plastic slat chair:** Seat 16½" wide x 12" deep

## KNITTED MEASUREMENTS

Circumference at feet: 70½"

Total length, including Backrest: 32½"

## YARN

JCA/Artful Yarns "Museum" (100% wool), super bulky singles

10 hanks (3.5oz/100g; 76yd/71m) in 5 ming vase (blue) OR 3 sister wendy (magenta)

## NEEDLES/TOOLS

US 15 (10mm) 24" long circular, or size to match gauge

Size P (10mm) crochet hook

4 stitch markers (one a different color for beg of rnd)

Tapestry needle

## GAUGE

7 sts and 10 rnds/rows = 4" in St st

Always check and MATCH gauge for best fit.

Drop/Latch next st; k2tog, knit to 2 sts before next marker, ssk; rep from * once—120 sts (4 sts decreased, 2 on each side section).

Rnds 11-19: Work even, sl m.

Rnds 20-39: Rep Rnds 10-19 twice—112 sts.

Rnd 40: Decrease Rnd—Drop/Latch first st, k28, Drop/Latch next st; k2tog, knit to next marker; Drop/Latch next st, k28, Drop/Latch next st; knit to 2 sts before next marker, ssk—110 sts, 30 sts between markers, Front and Back; 25 st each Side section.

Work even until piece measures 17½" from beg, or desired length to beg of Seat (approx 5 more rnds).

### SEAT

Beg Short Row Shaping (see page 171), in St st (knit on RS, purl on WS);

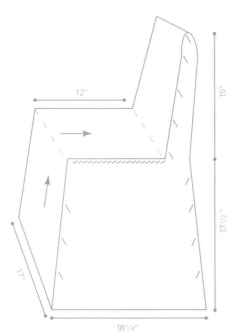

slip markers and cont to Drop/Latch seam sts every 10 rows as before.

K30 (Back); leave sts for Back on hold at this end of needle until you resume working rnds for Backrest.

Row 1: (RS) Shape Side sections— Knit to 2 sts before next marker, ssk (Left Side); k30 (Front); on Right Side, k2tog, wyif slip next st to RH needle, yb, turn.

Row 2: (WS) DO NOT return slipped st to RH needle as for Short Row wrap. P2tog (the 2 sts before the seam st); p30 (Front); on Left Side, p2tog, wyif slip next st to RH needle, yb, turn.

Row 3: Return slipped st to RH needle as for Short Row wrap, k1; k30 (Front); k1, wyif slip next st to RH needle, yb, turn.

Row 4: (WS) Rep Row 2.

Cont as established, rep Rows 1-4 until 19 sts have been decreased/30 rows have been worked—72 sts, 30 sts Front and Back; 6 sts each Side section; end WS row.

Work across to beg of rnd marker.

### BACKREST

Resume St st in rnds; sl m and cont to Drop/Latch seam sts every 10 rnds on Back and Front as before.

Shape Sides: Decrease Rnd—Dec 1 st each Side section as foll:

K30 (Back); knit to 2 sts before marker, ssk; k30 (Front); k2tog, knit to end.

Work even for 7 rnds.

Rep Decrease Rnd 3 times—64 sts, 30 sts Front and Back; 2 sts each Side section. Work even until Backrest measures 15"; piece measures 32½" from lower edge.

Work Decrease Rnd once more—1 st rem each Side section.

Bind off all sts on next rnd.

### FINISHING

Using Kitchener stitch, graft sts of Front and Back, including the seam sts (sandwich the rem Side st between them).

Edging: Using crochet hook and a double strand of yarn held to WS of piece (pull loops to RS while working across), working into 2 of every 3 cast on sts, work slip st around; fasten off.

Alternate Edging: If you don't feel comfortable crocheting, use tapestry needle and a double strand of yarn to work a chain st around lower edge.

# ballet t-shirt

## OVERVIEW

This T-shirt is worked in-the-round from the neck down without ever cutting yarn. Hold one strand (center-pull end) each from two skeins, rather than using both ends of one skein—you will be less likely to get into a tangle, plus for all sizes except the largest you'll have only the cast on and bind off ends to weave in. On the yoke, each round has four segments bordered by paired raglan increases: two wide segments, the Front and Back, and two shorter segments, the sleeves. Markers placed between each set of increases facilitate the shaping—be sure your marker for the beginning of the round (beg of rnd) is distinct from the increase (inc) markers, so that you don't mistakenly increase there. The beg of rnd is at the Back right sleeve raglan, and as that raglan increases it will become farther and farther away from the first increase marker. Keep in mind that when the instructions state to increase you will knit into front and back (k-f/b) of next stitch, so "inc" represents 1 stitch in terms of counting sts for that round. You will bind off the sleeve stitches between raglans for the top of the armhole and cast on new stitches for the underarm—your cast on and bind off tension will greatly affect stretch/size of openings. Each cast on or bound off stitch should exactly equal the width of each column of sts on the garment to ensure proper fit. Continuing in-the-round, you will create shaping marks running down the center Front and Back of the garment, starting just under the bust with mirrored decreases (dec) that flank the center stitch. The paired increases that will appear to align

## SIZES

**Girl's:** Small (2T–3T) (Medium [4–5 year])

**Woman's:** Small/Medium (Medium/Large)

*Note that fabric is very stretchy when choosing size.*

**Shown in Girl's Medium and Woman's Small/ Medium.**

## KNITTED MEASUREMENTS

**Girl's:** Chest 18¼ (20½)"

**Woman's:** Chest 25½ (28¾)"

## YARN

Brown Sheep's "Cotton Fleece" (80% cotton/ 20% merino), 24-ply worsted (use double strand)

**Girl's:** 2 (2) skeins (3.5oz/ 100g; 215yd/200m) in 220 provincial rose

**Woman's:** 2 (3) skeins in 100 cotton ball

## NEEDLES/TOOLS

**Girl's:** US 10½ (6.5mm) 16" long circular, or size to match gauge

**Woman's:** US 15 (10mm) 24" long circular, or size to match gauge

5 stitch markers (one a different color for beginning of round)

## GAUGE

**Girl's:** 14 sts and 20 rnds = 4" in St st using smaller needles and 2 strands held together

**Woman's:** 10 sts and 12 rnds = 4" in St st using larger needles and 2 strands held together

Always check and MATCH gauge for best fit.

below are actually worked on the first 2 sts of the trio. The k-f/b increase creates a bar to left of the old stitch, so for the illusion of a center Front stitch you need to increase into the stitch before and then into the center stitch. You may find it helpful to tie a marker on the center Front and Back neck stitch of the first round and eyeball the stitch column to make sure marks are aligned.

*Note: There are 2 sets of numbers in the instructions; using appropriate needle size, work using the first set of numbers for the smaller sizes given (for girl's and woman's) and the second set for the larger sizes.*

### YOKE

Using appropriate needle size, longtail cast-on method, and 2 strands of yarn held together, cast on 56 (62) sts. Pm of a distinct color on RH needle for beg of rnd. Join, being careful not to twist sts (see page 171). Beg St st (knit every rnd).

**Rounds 1 and 2:** Knit even.

### Shape Raglan

**Rnd 3:** Increase Rnd—Inc (k-f/b), pm; inc, k7 (8), inc, pm; inc, k17 (19), inc, pm; inc, k7 (8), inc, pm; inc, k17 (19)—64 (70) sts [8 sts inc].

**Rnd 4:** Knit even, slipping markers (sl m).

**Rnd 5:** Increase Rnd—* Knit to one st before inc marker, inc, sl m, inc; rep from * 3 times, knit to end of rnd—72 (78) sts.

**Rnd 6:** Knit even, sl m.

Rep Rnds 5 and 6 until a total of 5 Increase Rnds have been worked, ending Rnd 11 (Increase Rnd)—96 (102) sts.

**Rnd 12:** Knit even, sl m.

### Divide for Armholes

**Rnd 13:** K7, bind off 19 (20) sts for Sleeve; counting st on RH needle (st rem after bind-off) as the first st, k29 (31) for Front; bind off 19 (20) sts for Sleeve; k29 (31) for Back. (*Note: This goes beyond marker at beg of rnd; remove marker, pm at new beg of rnd.*)—58 (62) sts.

### Shape Underarm

**Rnd 14:** Using single cast-on method (wrap yarn around thumb and place loop on needle), cast on 3 (5) for underarm, k29 (31) for Front, cast on 3 (5) for underarm, k29 (31) for Back—64 (72) sts.

**Rnds 15–24:** Knit even.

### Shape Front and Back Bodice

**Rnd 25:** K3 (5) [underarm], k12 (13), ssk, k1 [center Front st], k2tog, k27 (31), ssk, k1 [center Back st], k2tog, knit to end of rnd—60 (68) sts.

**Rnds 26–31:** Knit even.

**Rnd 32:** Increase Rnd—K15 (18), inc, pm, inc (in center Front st), k28 (32), inc, pm, inc (in center Back st); knit to end of rnd—64 (72) sts.

**Rnds 33–35:** Knit even.

Cont as established, inc one st each side of Front and Back markers every fourth rnd 4 times more—80 (88) sts.

**Rnds 49–51:** Knit even. For larger size, or for a less cropped look, knit an additional 3 rounds (6 rounds total).

Bind off all sts loosely.

Weave in ends.

Block lightly.

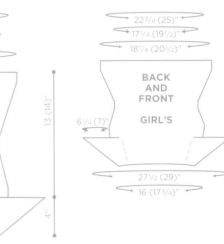

# yoke vest

## SPECIAL TECHNIQUE

**Mirrored decreases each side of a center st:** * Knit to 2 sts before marker, work left-slanting dec, slip marker (sl m), k1, sl m, work right-slanting dec—2 sts decreased, 1 each side of center st.

**Mirrored increases:** Work to one st before marker, inc (k-f/b), sl m, then inc in next (center) st—2 sts increased, one each side of center st.

## BODY

Using long-tail cast-on method and appropriate needle size, cast on 86 sts. Pm on RH needle for beg of rnd. Join, being careful not to twist sts (see page 171).

**Rnds 1–6:** Knit even.

**Rnd 7:** Decrease Rnd—K19, * left-slanting dec, pm, k1, pm, right-slanting dec *, k38, rep between *'s once, knit to end of rnd—82 sts.

**Rnds 8–10:** Knit even, sl m.

**Rnd 11:** Decrease Rnd—* Knit to 2 sts before marker, left-slanting dec, sl m, k1, sl m, right-slanting dec; rep from * once, knit to end of rnd—78 sts.

Knit even for 3 rnds, sl m.

**Rnds 15–32:** Cont as established, rep Rnds 11–14; a total of 6 Decrease Rnds—62 sts.

## SIZES

Small/Medium (Large)
*Note that fabric is very stretchy when choosing size.*
**Shown in Small/Medium.**

## KNITTED MEASUREMENTS

Chest/Hip: 28 ²/₃ (34 ½)"
Waist: 20 ²/₃ (24 ¾)"

## YARN

Needful Yarns/Filtes King "Van Dyck" (46% wool/39% acrylic/15% alpaca), 8-ply bulky

3 (4) balls (3.5oz/100g; 117yd/107m) in 129 burgundy heather

## NEEDLES/TOOLS

**Size Small/Medium:** US 11 (8mm) 24" long circular, or size to match gauge
**Size Large:** US 13 (9mm) 24" long circular, or size to match gauge

5 stitch markers (one a different color for beg of rnd)

## GAUGE

**Size Small/Medium:** 12 sts and 16 rnds (rows) = 4" in St st using smaller needle
**Size Large:** 10 sts and 14 rnds (rows) = 4" in St st using larger needle
Always check and MATCH gauge for best fit.

Piece should measure 8 (9)" from the beg.

** Next Rnd: Increase Rnd—* Knit to one st before next marker, inc, sl m, inc (discard this next marker—the incs will push it farther away from center st; will place new marker for dec later); rep from * once, knit to end of rnd—66 sts.

Knit even for 3 rnds, sl m.

Cont as established, rep from ** twice, then work Increase Rnd once more; a total of 4 Increase Rnds—78 sts.

Knit even for 1 rnd.

Cont to inc every fourth rnd as established, for a total of 6 times, AT SAME TIME, beg working Front and Back in rows as foll:

### Divide for Armholes

Row 1: (RS) * Sl 1 (selvedge st at armhole), left-slanting dec, k33, right-slanting dec, k1—(39 sts dec to 37 sts); leave yarn hanging, ready for

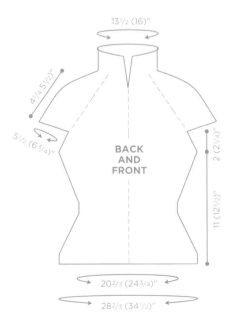

13½ (16)"

4¼ (5½)"

5½ (6¾)"

BACK AND FRONT

2 (2¼)"

11 (12½)"

20⅔ (24¾)"

28⅔ (34½)"

WS row on Front; join new ball of yarn, rep from * for Back.

Cont to work Front and Back with separate balls as foll:

Row 2 and all WS rows through Row 8: Sl 1, purl to end.

Row 3: Sl 1, left-slanting dec, knit to one st before next marker, inc, sl m, inc, knit to last 3 sts of this side, right-slanting dec, k1—37 sts.

Row 5: Sl 1, left-slanting dec, k33, right-slanting dec, k1—35 sts.

Row 7: Sl 1, left-slanting dec, knit to one st before next marker, inc, sl m, inc, knit to last 3 sts of this side, right-slanting dec, k1—35 sts.

Row 9: Work across sts of Front. Using single cast-on method (wrap yarn around thumb and place loop on needle), cast on 17 sts over armhole opening, work across sts of Back, cast on 17 sts over armhole—104 sts.

### YOKE

Pm for beg of rnd (at Back left shoulder), join and knit even for 6 rnds.

Rnd 7: K2, left-slanting dec, pm, k1, pm, right-slanting dec, k8, left-slanting dec, slip first marker for center Front, k1, place second marker for center Front, right-slanting dec, * k8, left-slanting dec, pm, k1, pm, right-slanting dec; rep from * until 8 pairs of decs have been worked, ending last rep with k6—88 sts.

(The 2 sts at beg of rnd make segment equal; Yoke is an octagon—8 segments of 12 sts decreased to 10, with one st separating each segment; the center Front and Back decs should be aligned with those worked on Body.)

Knit even for 3 rnds.

Rnd 11: K1, left-slanting dec, sl m, k1, sl m, right-slanting dec, k6, left-slanting

dec, sl first marker for center Front, k1, sl second marker for center Front, right-slanting dec, * k6, left-slanting dec, sl m, k1, sl m, right-slanting dec; rep from * until 8 pairs of decs have been worked, ending last rep with k5. (The st at the beg of rnd makes segment equal—as sts dec the beg of rnd will change, so remove that marker and use Back left shoulder as reference for beg of rnd)—72 sts.

Knit even for 3 rnds.

Rnd 15: Work decs as established to either side of markers—56 sts.

Knit even for 3 rnds.

Rnd 19: Work decs as established to either side of markers—40 sts; 8 segments of 4 sts, with one st in between each segment.

### Divide for Neck

Knit to center Front st and work a right-slanting dec (the center st will lie under the st to its left and the yarn extends from the loop of the center st), pm for center neck; do not cont on RS row, but in order to create balanced loop through center st at bottom neck, turn so WS of fabric is facing and purl WS row to right neck edge, turn, knit to left edge, turn, and purl 1 row.

Next RS row: Starting at right neck edge, work dec as foll:

K2, work [left-slanting dec, sl m, k1, sl m, right-slanting dec] 6 times, ending last rep at left neck edge with k2—25 sts. Turn; purl WS row.

Next Row: Inc into st before each marker around—39 sts. Work in rows of St st for 2½" more. Bind off loosely.

# ruffled gloves

**TIPS**

I use smooth waste yarn to hold sts in small curved areas, as on this glove. St holders aren't as flexible, so they may allow sts to escape or stretch out sts at the edges. If you have a fifth needle in your smaller set of dpns, you can create a shorter set of dpns, which will make it more convenient to knit each finger in the rnd. Cut the needle into 3 pieces, each about 2" long, and use a sheet of sandpaper or emery board to smooth the ends into points. Use 2 of the needles to hold the sts and the third one as the working needle, or combine the shorter needles with 1 of the longer dpn.

**RUFFLED CUFF**

Using smaller dpn and long-tail cast-on method, cast on 40 sts. Pm on RH needle for beg of round. Distribute sts evenly on 3 dpn; join, being careful not to twist sts. Beg 2x2 Rib; work 2 rnds even, then work from ** to ** below 3 times.

** **Rnds 1 and 2:** Using smaller dpn, work even in 2x2 Rib.

**Rnds 3–6:** Change to larger dpn and St st; work even.

**Rnd 7:** Fold Line—Knit, wrapping yarn twice around needle for each st. (This will create elongated sts; on next rnd, drop the extra loops as you work around.)

**Rnds 8–10:** Cont with larger dpn, work even.

**Rnd 11:** Ruffle—(You will be working into the front loops of the sts on the dpn, and into loops on the WS from rnds below to fold fabric into ruffled "hem.") Insert working needle knitwise into next st, then peer over top of needle into the center of the piece so that the sts on the WS are visible;

## SIZE
Woman's Medium

## KNITTED
## MEASUREMENTS
7" around palm; adjust finger length by trying on

## YARN
Jaeger "Luxury Tweed" (65% merino lambswool/ 35% alpaca), 2-ply DK

2 balls (1.75oz/50g; 195yd/ 180m) in 825 lavendula

## NEEDLES/TOOLS
US 3 (3.25mm) set of 4 or 5 double-pointed needles (dpn), or size to match gauge

US 6 (4.25mm) set of 4 or 5 double-pointed needles (dpn) for ruffles

Smooth waste yarn

Stitch marker

Tapestry needle

## GAUGE
24 sts and 28 rnds = 4" in St st using smaller needles

Always check and MATCH gauge for best fit.

pick up a loop on the WS (directly below the st on the needle) in Rnd 2—the last rnd of Rib; knit the st on the dpn and the loop tog. Staggering the rnds that the loops are picked up on, from Rnd 1 to Rnd 5, to create an uneven edge on Ruffle, cont working next st tog with a loop from the WS around entire Cuff.

Change to smaller dpn **.

After working a total of 3 ruffles, cont with smaller dpn in 2x2 Rib for desired length to end of wrist—2½" more for shorter glove, 5" more for longer glove.

**Next Rnd:** Cont with smaller dpn, change to St st.

Work even for 4 rnds.

### THUMB GUSSET

Inc 1 st each side of Thumb every other rnd 9 times as foll:

K19, pm, inc (k-f/b), inc, knit to end.

Work even for 1 rnd, sl m.

**Next Rnd:** Knit to marker, sl m, inc, k2, inc, knit to end of rnd.

Work even for 1 rnd, sl m.

**Next Rnd:** Knit to marker, sl m, inc, k3, inc, knit to end of rnd.

Cont as established (inc 2 sts EOR, working 1 st more between the first and second inc each time), until there are 18 sts between the inc bars for Thumb.

### PALM

**Next Rnd:** Cont in St st, knit around to Thumb sts, run a piece of scrap yarn through Thumb sts (to hold), pm for beg of rnd; cast on 2 sts above where sts are on hold for Thumb—42 sts. Work even for 1¾" or desired length to base of fingers—try it on.

### INDEX FINGER

Place 5 sts before marker onto dpn, k2 (the sts above Thumb); with another dpn, k5, then cast on 2 sts—14 sts; run scrap yarn through palm sts to hold and free up dpn if necessary. Using third dpn, cont in St st, work even until finger measures 2¾" or desired length—about ¼" from finger tip—try it on.

**Next Rnd:** Decrease Rnd—K2tog around—7 sts.

Cut yarn leaving 4" tail, thread tail onto tapestry needle, run through sts of last rnd and pull to secure, weave in end on WS.

### MIDDLE FINGER

Place 5 sts to the right of Index finger onto dpn, knit these sts with another dpn, then cast on 2 sts in the space between Index and Middle finger; k5 at other side of hand, then cast on 2 sts in the space between Middle

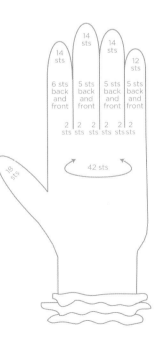

finger and Ring finger—14 sts. Work as for Index finger until finger measures 3¼" or desired length; work Decrease Rnd, then finish as for Index finger.

### RING FINGER

Place 5 sts to the right of Middle finger onto dpn, knit these with another dpn, then cast on 2 sts in the space between Middle finger and Ring finger; k5 at other side of hand, then cast on 2 sts in the space between Ring finger and Pinky—14 sts. Work as for Index finger until finger measures 3" or desired length; work Decrease Rnd, then finish as for Index finger.

### PINKY FINGER

Place 5 sts to the right of Ring finger onto dpn, knit these with another dpn; then cast on 2 sts in the space between Ring finger and Pinky; k5 at other side of hand—12 sts. Work as for Index finger until finger measures 2½" or desired length; k2tog around—6 sts. Finish as for Index finger.

### THUMB

Place 18 sts on hold for Thumb onto 2 dpn. Work as for Index finger until Thumb measures 2¼" or desired length; k2tog around—9 sts. Finish as for Index finger.

### FINISHING

Graft cast on sts between fingers together.

# felted tweed hat

**SIZE**
Woman's Medium

**KNITTED
MEASUREMENTS**
Before felting, 24" circum-
ference/5" tall crown; after
felting 22" circumference/
4" tall crown

**YARN**
Jaeger "Luxury Tweed"
(65% merino lambswool/
35% alpaca), 2-ply DK
(use double strand as
indicated in instructions)

2 balls (1.75oz/50g;
195yd/180m) each in 823
fern (A) and 826 kew green
(B), plus small amount
829 red robin (C)

**NEEDLES/TOOLS**
US 9 (5.5mm) 16" and 24"
long circular, or size to
match gauge

Stitch marker

Tapestry needle

**NOTIONS**
1 yd ¾"-wide velvet ribbon

Sewing needle and thread to
match A for felted flower
pieces

**GAUGE**
**Before felting:** 17 sts and 22
rows = 4" in St st or Irish
Moss using 2 strands held
together

**After felting:** 18 sts and 26
rows = 4" in St st or Irish
Moss using 2 strands held
together

Always check and MATCH
gauge for best fit.

## SPECIAL TECHNIQUE
**Felting:** Place pieces in washing
machine with an old towel or two;
set temperature for hot wash,
cold rinse; add small amount of
mild detergent. Two cycles should
produce the desired degree of
felting; check swatches/hat after
first cycle.

Straighten edges of swatches to
5" x 5" square. Dry flat.

Dry hat on a hat stand or inverted
bowl in the desired hat size, pulling
and shaping as it dries.

### Short Row Shaping
(see page 171)

### Irish Moss (Double Seed) St (even
number sts)

Rnds/Rows 1 and 2: * K1, p1; rep from
* around/across.

Rnds/Rows 3 and 4: * P1, k1; rep from
* around/across.

Rep Rnds/Rows 1–4 for Irish Moss.

## GAUGE SWATCHES/
## FLOWER TRIM
Make three pieces that will measure
5" x 5" after felting; these can be
used as gauge swatches as well.

Using shorter circular needle, long-
tail cast-on method, and 2 strands
of indicated color held together, cast
on 22 sts. Working back and forth in
rows, with A, work in Irish Moss; with
B, work in St st; with C, work in St st;
work even until piece measures 6"
from beg. Bind off all sts. Felt
swatches (see above).

## CROWN
Using shorter circular needle, long-
tail cast-on method, and 1 strand
each of color A and B held together,
cast on 100 sts. Pm on RH needle for

beg of rnd. Join, being careful not to twist sts (see page 171).

Beg Irish Moss; work even until piece measures 3" from beg.

**Shape Crown:** First Decrease Rnd—Cont in patt as established, dec 10 sts evenly around as foll:

* Work 16 sts, dec twice (k2tog if sts are k1, p1; p2tog if sts are p1, k1); rep from * around—90 sts.

Work even for 1".

**Second Decrease Rnd:** * Work 14 sts, dec twice; rep from * around—80 sts. Work even until piece measures 5" from beg.

### SHAPE TOP OF CROWN

Beg Short Row Shaping (each Short Row is composed of a RS row and a WS row) in St st and as foll:

**Short Row 1:** (RS) K7, wrp-t; (WS) p7, wrp-t.

**Short Row 2:** K8 (7 sts plus the wrapped st from last RS row), wrp-t; p9, (8 sts of previous row plus wrapped st from last WS row), wrp-t.

**Short Row 3:** K10 (9 sts plus the wrapped st from last RS row), wrp-t; p11 (10 sts of previous row plus wrapped st from last WS row); wrp-t.

Cont in this manner until 6 Crown sts have been incorporated at each side—19 sts for Top of Crown.

Cont to work across Top with this width—19 sts.

Decrease Crown sts tog with Top sts at each side as foll:

**Short Row 1:** (RS) K18, k2tog (the Top st with next wrapped Crown st), wrp-t; (WS) p18, p2tog (the Top st with next wrapped Crown st), wrp-t.

Cont in this manner until 38 sts rem—19 Top sts plus 19 Crown sts.

Decrease the Top sts while incorporating the crown sts as foll:

**Short Row 1:** (RS) K18, k2tog (the Top st with next wrapped Crown st), wrp-t; (WS) p2tog (decreases Top st), p16, p2tog (the Top st with next wrapped Crown st), wrp-t.

**Short Row 2:** K2tog (decreases Top st), k15, k2tog (the Top st with next wrapped Crown st), wrp-t; p2tog (decreases Top st), p13, p2tog (the Top st with next wrp Crown st), wrp-t.

Cont to dec as established at each side until 7 Top sts and 7 Crown sts rem.

Using tapestry needle, 1 strand each of colors A and B, and Kitchener st, graft rem sts together.

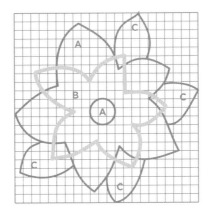

Enlarge Grid to 4½" (approximately 250%); make 3 copies. (Each square will equal about ⅕".) Cut out each piece and use as a template according to instructions.

### BRIM

Using shorter circular needle, beg at Back of hat (beg of Crown rnd), pick up and knit 100 sts around cast on edge. Pm on RH needle for beg of round. Join; beg St st. Change to longer needle when sts become crowded.

**Rnd 1:** Increase Rnd—* K8, inc in next 2 sts (k-f/b); rep from * around —120 sts.

**Rnds 2 and 3:** Work even.

Rep Rnds 1–3 four times more, working 2 more sts between double inc each time—200 sts.

Bind off all sts loosely.

### FINISHING

**Flowers:** Using A swatch and Grid (see left), cut out a large 5-petal flower, plus the circle for flower center; using B swatch, cut out a small 5-petaled flower; using C swatch, cut 4 separate leaf shapes. Layer flower center over small flower, over large flower, arranged as shown and, using sewing needle and thread, tack through all layers at center, leaving edges open. Sew leaf pieces to edge of large flower on WS.

**Ribbon:** Using tapestry needle and 2 strands of A, lay ribbon around the lower edge of the crown (where the brim meets it); bring tapestry needle up from WS to RS through pick up rnd, then from RS to WS over top of ribbon; secure ribbon in this manner, spacing sts ½" apart. Pull ribbon to shape hat to wearer's head, then tie and let ends hang as I did or cut ends and sew ribbon ends together. Attach felted flower.

# puff sleeve bolero

## OVERVIEW

The sweater Back is knit from bottom up, then Fronts (which do not extend to shoulder but merely attach to Sleeve at underarm) are picked up and knit from side to center Front. Ribbed bands worked with an increase ruffle effect border all pieces. The top band draws in the neck and shoulders and finishes the top and Front edge of Sleeve caps; the lower edging curves up each Front.

## BACK

Using smaller needle and A, cast on 41 (45, 49) sts. Beg 1x1 Rib; work even until piece measures 5" from beg, end with a WS row.

**Shape Armhole:** Cont in Rib, dec 1 st each side EOR 4 times—33 (37, 41) sts. Work even until armhole measures 7" from beg of shaping; place all sts on holder.

## RIGHT FRONT

With RS of Back facing, using smaller needle and A, pick up and knit 15 sts along side from lower edge to armhole (skip every 3rd row). Change to larger needle, join a strand B (one strand of each yarn held together) and beg St st.

(WS) Purl. Cont as established, work even until piece measures 7 (7 ³/₄, 8 ½)" from pick up row; place all sts on holder.

## LEFT FRONT

Work as for Right Front, beg at armhole, working to lower edge. Work even until piece measures 7 (7 ³/₄, 8 ½)" from pick up row. Cut strand of B (one strand of A rem); do not place sts on holder.

## FRONT/BANDS AND LOWER EDGING

(RS) Change to smaller needle; using 1 strand A, knit 14 sts of Left Front; in 15th st inc 2 (knit into front, back, front of st) to form a rounded corner; pick up and knit 14 (16, 18) sts evenly spaced along lower edge of Left Front (skip 3 rows across), pick up and knit 39 (43, 47) sts evenly along lower edge of Back, then pick up and knit 14 (16, 18) sts evenly along lower edge of Right Front as for Left Front;

## SIZES

Small (Medium, Large)
**Shown in size Medium.**

## KNITTED MEASUREMENTS

**Chest (closed):** 32 (35, 38)"
**Length:** 15"

## YARN

Needful Yarns/King "Super" (100% merino), bulky; 12 cabled 2-ply strands
4 (4, 5) balls (3.5oz/100g; 128yd/117m) in 1694 blue (A)

Needful Yarns/King "Extra" (100% merino), worsted; 8 cabled 2-ply strands
2 (2, 3) balls (1.75oz/50g; 128yd/117m) in 1694 blue (B)

## NEEDLES/TOOLS

US 10 ½ (6.5mm) 32" long circular, or size to match gauge
US 17 (12mm) circular or straight
Stitch holders/spare circular needles
Tapestry needle

## NOTIONS

1 ½" plastic ring for making Dorset button

## GAUGE

10 sts and 18 rows = 4" in 1x1 Rib, using smaller needle and A, slightly stretched
8 sts and 10 rows = 4" in St st using larger needle and one strand each A and B held together
Always check and MATCH gauge for best fit.

inc 2 in first st on holder to form a rounded corner, knit rem 14 sts from Right Front holder—101 (109, 117) sts.

(WS) Change to 1x1 Rib, beg and end p1; work even for 2 rows more.

**Buttonhole Row:** (RS) Work as established to 6 sts from the end, bind off 3 sts, work to end.

(WS) Rib 3, cast on 3 sts, work in Rib to end.

Cont in Rib, work even for 2 more rows.

**Ruffle:** (RS) * K-f/b, p1; rep from * to last st, k1 (do not inc in last st)—151 (163, 175) sts.

(WS) * P1, k2; rep from * to last st, p1.

(RS) Bind off all sts knitwise.

### SLEEVE

Using smaller needle and 1 strand A, cast on 21 (23, 27) sts; beg 1x1 Rib.

**Shape Lower Sleeve:** Inc 1 st each side every 12th row 3 times—27 (29, 33) sts. Work even until piece measures 11" from beg, end with a RS row.

**Shape Upper Sleeve:** (WS) Inc 10 sts evenly across this row—37 (39, 43) sts.

(RS) Change to larger needles, join a strand of B and beg St st; work even until upper sleeve measures 6" from inc row, end with a WS row.

**Shape Sleeve Cap:** Dec 1 st each side every row 4 times—29 (31, 35) sts.

Work even for 3" (cap measures 5" from beg of shaping); end with a WS row.

(RS) * K2tog; rep from * to last st, k1—15 (16, 18) sts.

**Right Sleeve:** (WS) Bind off 4 sts, knit to end; place rem 11 (12, 14) sts on holder.

**Left Sleeve:** (WS) Purl 1 row, turn. Bind off 4 sts, place rem 11 (12, 14) sts on holder.

### CUFF RUFFLE

With RS facing, using smaller needle and 1 strand A, pick up and knit 23 (25, 27) sts along lower edge of sleeve.

(WS) Change to 1x1 Rib, beg and end p1; work 1 row even.

(RS) * K-f/b, p1; rep from * to last st, k1, (do not inc in last st)—34 (37, 40) sts.

(WS) * P1, k2; rep from * to last st, p1.

(RS) Bind off all sts knitwise.

### FINISHING

Sew sleeve seam, using tapestry needle and 1 strand of B.

**Sleeve Cap:** Sew Cap to armhole edge at Back, incorporating the length of the Cap plus the 4 bound-off sts at top Cap; sew front of Sleeve Cap to top edge of Front for 3", leaving the rem open. (On the Sleeve Cap, there will be an open edge of 2½" before sts on holder.)

### TOP BAND

With RS facing, beg at Right Front upper edge, just after Front button band, using smaller needle and 1 strand A, pick up and knit 10 (12, 14) sts along Right Front to where it meets the Sleeve Cap; knit 11 (12, 14) sts from Right Sleeve holder; knit across 33 (37, 41) sts from Back holder; knit 11 (12, 14) sts from Left Sleeve holder, 10 (12, 14) sts along top edge of Left Front, ending at Front button band—75 (85, 97) sts.

(WS) Change to 1x1 Rib, beg and end p1; work 1 row even.

(RS) * K-f/b, p1; rep from * to last st, k1 (do not inc in last st)—112 (130, 148) sts.

(WS) * P1, k2; rep from * to last st, p1.

(RS) Bind off all sts knitwise.

### DORSET BUTTON

Tie a 36" long strand of A to the plastic ring, thread other end on tapestry needle. Wrap yarn around plastic ring until edge is completely covered. Then make 8 equidistant spokes around ring that are crossed in the center (think God's-eye) to cover its length completely and close up the surrounding space. When all eight spokes are covered, run yarn through to center back of button, sew to Left Front, opposite buttonhole. Both sides of the button are attractive; I chose the one that looks like a rose, rather than the one that looks like wagon wheel.

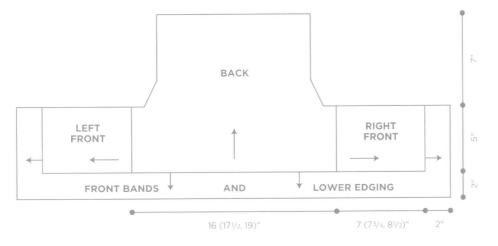

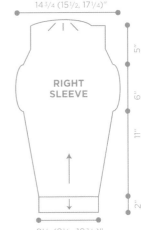

# "cast-away" fringe pullover

## SPECIAL TECHNIQUE

**Cast-Away Fringe:** Curved, fringed hems are formed by casting on and binding off extra sts at the end of each row. You always begin at the lowest dip of the curve working fringes outward, always spaced every 3 sts, but bottom hem fringes are 2 sts longer than neck and sleeve fringes. When making fringe use single cast-on—long-tail cast-on is too thick. Cast on the number of sts required for the fringe, plus 3 for the "hem" at the end of the rows, with the needle held in right hand. Then turn, placing needle in left hand and bind off fringe sts at beg of next row (knitwise when RS is facing, purlwise when WS is facing). Note that to bind off the final fringe st you will use 1 st that will remain on the RH needle for the "hem."

## BODY

Cast on 90 (96, 102) sts gradually, while creating a curved hem with fringe between every 3 sts as foll:

Cast on 18 sts, turn; bind off 15 sts knitwise (one st has been knit in order to bind off last st and is on RH needle), k2 rem sts—3 sts cast on; first fringe created.

Cast on 15 sts, turn; bind off 15 purlwise, p3—second fringe created.

Cast on 18 sts, turn; bind off 15 knitwise, k5 rem sts—6 sts cast on; 3 fringes.

Cast on 18 sts, turn; bind off 15 purlwise, purl to end—9 sts cast on; 4 fringes.

Cont in this manner until 39 sts have been cast on and 14 fringes have been created. (Last fringe was made on a WS row, completing hem shaping.)

With WS facing, cast on 3 sts, turn.

(RS) Knit across 42 cast on sts. The rem sts will be cast on with RS of piece facing and no further shaping.

Cont from the end of this (RS) row, cast on and create fringes as foll:

*Cast on 18 sts, turn; bind off 15, turn.

Rep from * until 48 (54, 60) additional sts have been cast on and 16 (18, 20) additional fringes created—90 (96, 102) sts.

## SIZES

Small (Medium, Large)
**Shown in Small (black pearl) and Medium (chino).**

## KNITTED MEASUREMENTS

**Chest:** 35⅓ (37⅓, 39⅓)"
**Length:** 22½" on Right Front, with an extra 3½" dip on Left Front
**Sleeve at upper arm:** 14 (15, 16)"

## YARN

Lorna's Laces "Revelation" (100% wool), bulky singles with 2-ply binder

6 (6, 7) hanks (4oz/114g; 125yd/115m) in 15 chino OR 27 black pearl

## NEEDLES/TOOLS

US 10½ (6.5mm) 28" or 32" long circular, or size to match gauge

Stitch markers

Stitch holders/spare circular needles

Tapestry needle

## GAUGE

12 sts and 16 rows = 4" in St st (this yarn varies thick to thin so sample various areas of gauge swatch).

Always check and MATCH gauge for best fit.

**Joining Rnd:** Join, being careful not to twist sts. Beg St st (knit every rnd); k12 (15, 18), pm (left side seam and new beg of rnd—so that extra length of hem will be placed properly over left front); k45 (48, 51), pm (right side seam); knit to end. Work even, slipping markers (sl m), until piece measures 5″ from Joining Rnd.

**Shape Torso:** Increase Rnd—Inc (k-f/b), knit to 1 st before side marker, inc; sl m, inc, knit to last st, inc—94 (100, 106) sts.

Cont to inc in the sts before and after each marker every 6th rnd 3 more times—106 (112, 118) sts. When piece measures 13″ from edge of hem at right side seam, place sts on holders and spare needle as foll:

Place 3 sts each side of both seam markers on separate holders for underarms (6 sts each holder); place rem sts on spare needle (47 [50, 53] sts each for Back and Front).

## SLEEVES

Cast on 27 sts gradually while creating a fringe between every 3 sts as foll:

Cast on 16 sts, turn; bind off 13 knitwise (one st has been knit in order to bind off the last st and is on RH needle), k2 rem sts—3 sts cast on; 1 fringe created.

Cast on 13 sts, turn; bind off 13 purlwise, p3—second fringe created.

Cast on 16 sts, turn; bind off 13 knitwise, k5 rem sts—6 sts cast on; 3 fringes.

Cont in this manner until 24 sts have been cast on; 9 fringes created.

Cast on 3 sts—27 sts.

Beg St st; work even in rows until piece measures 3″ from cast on edge.

**Shape Sleeve:** Inc 1 st each side every fourth row 7 (9, 11) times—41 (45, 49) sts. When piece measures 17½″ from top of hem, end with WS row; bind off 3 sts at beg next 2 rows. Place rem sts on holder or spare needle. Work another sleeve in same manner, working the bind offs but do not place on holder or cut yarn; turn piece RS facing.

## YOKE

**Joining Rnd:** (RS) Work across 35 (39, 43) sts of Sleeve, pm; take up body piece, work across 47 (50, 53) sts of Front, pm; work across sts of rem Sleeve, pm; then work across 47 (50, 53) sts of Back—164 (178, 192) sts. Pm for beg of rnd.

**Raglan Shaping:** Dec 1 st each side of markers every other rnd 11 (12, 13) times as foll:

**Decrease Rnd:** Slipping markers, * K2, ssk, work to 4 sts before next marker, k2tog, k2; rep from * 3 times—8 sts decreased.

After all dec rnds are worked, yoke will measures 5½ (6, 6½)″ from Joining Rnd—76 (82, 88) sts. Bind off all sts loosely.

## COLLAR

Cast on 81 (87, 93) sts gradually while creating a fringe between every 3 sts, working as for sleeve until 24 sts cast on and 9 fringes created.

(RS) (The rem sts will be cast on with RS of piece facing and no further shaping.) Cont from the end of this (RS) row, cast on and create fringes as foll:

* Cast on 16 sts, turn; bind off 13, turn.

Rep from * 17 (19, 21) times, turn.

Cast on 3 sts—81 (87, 93) sts. Pm on RH needle for beg of rnd. Join, being careful not to twist sts.

Work even in St st until piece measures 5″ from straight side of hem.

**Next Rnd:** Dec 5 sts evenly around—76 (82, 88) sts.

Work even for 3″ more; bind off all sts loosely.

## FINISHING

With RS of garment facing WS of Collar, align bound off edges; the beg of Collar bind off rnd meets beg of sweater bind off rnd at Back left sleeve. Graft sts together easing in extra sts of Collar. Fold Collar to Front so RS is facing.

*Note: Collar falls loosely over shoulders; to wear gathered around neck (as shown on page 30), run a length of cording or yarn around Collar seam and tie.*

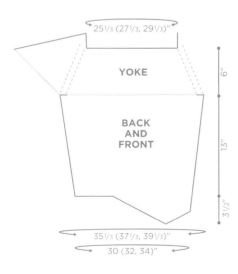

# dreamcatcher medallion cardigan

## OVERVIEW
This cardigan is worked in one piece from ribbed waistband to armholes, but is divided at Back to shape the medallion circle that will later be filled in by picking up around the edge with a circular needle and working into the center. Read instructions carefully before beg; the dart and side shaping, buttonholes, and Back opening are all worked at the same time. When you reach the beg of the armholes, you may want to finish the Fronts before resuming Back pieces—or challenge yourself to work the top of the medallion, armhole shaping, and Front neck shaping simultaneously as I did. I jotted down each row then checked them off. You may also find it helpful to graph out the decreases and bind offs of the Back medallion that are written out in the instructions. You may use any style of decrease—I alternated between left- and right-slanting along each edge to keep it stable. For a cleaner medallion outline, when picking up sts, be sure to do so outside of any visible decrease line or selvedge st. When working the Medallion opening on the Back, Right side edge comes "first" on RS rows, Left side edge "first" on WS rows; bind offs can only be done at the beg of a row, so cannot be done on first edge, which is continuation of piece; simple cast on can be done at each edge, on same row by making a loop on RH or LH needle as needed.

## BODY
Using longer needle and long-tail cast-on method, cast on 151 (163, 175, 187) sts; beg 1x1 Rib. (WS) * K1, p1; rep from * to last st, k1. Cont in 1x1 Rib until piece measures ½" from beg, end with WS row.

**Buttonhole:** Cont in Rib, on Right Front band work 3-row buttonhole as foll:

**Row 1:** (RS) P1, k1, yo, k2tog, work to end.

**Row 2:** (WS) Work across to yo from previous row, yo, drop yo from last row, p1, k1.

**Row 3:** (RS) P1, k1, drop yo and place both yo's onto LH needle, purl them tog, work to end.

You will cont to make a total of 6 buttonholes in the same manner with 13 rows between the end of one buttonhole and beg of the next (spaced about 2″ apart). The next buttonhole should be worked on the 4th row after the Rib waistband.

Work even in Rib until piece measures 2½″ from beg, end with RS row.

### Establish Patt and Side Seams:

**Row 1:** (WS) Work 5 sts in Rib, beg St st; work 34 (37, 40, 43) more sts for Left Front, pm; cont in St st, work 73 (79, 85, 91) sts for Back, pm; work to last 5 sts, work in Rib to end for Right Front—each Front has 39 (42, 45, 48) sts. (From this point, WS rows will have odd numbers and RS rows even numbers.)

**Rows 2–5:** Cont buttonholes and patt as established, slipping markers (sl m), work even for 4 rows.

**Row 6:** (RS) Begin Dart and Side Shaping—Work 17 (19, 21, 23) sts, pm for dart; inc (k-f/b), work to seam marker (21 [22, 23, 24] sts), sl m; inc, work 71 (77, 83, 89), inc, sl m; work 20 (21, 22, 23) sts, inc, pm for dart; work to end. Slipping markers, cont to inc every 6th row 8 times total, working incs on st after first and 2nd markers and on st before 3rd and 4th markers each time for directional

effect (darts will be vertical). After last inc row has been worked, discard the dart markers; keep the side markers in place, AT SAME TIME, when piece measures 5½″, end with WS row—163 (175, 187, 199) sts; 79 (85, 91, 97) sts between markers for Back.

### Beg Medallion opening on Back:
(The circle will be 10″ in diameter, 51 sts wide and 72 rows high.)

**Row 22:** (RS) Work across right Front; work 34 (37, 40, 43) sts of Back, join new ball of yarn and bind off 11 sts, work to end. Working both sides at same time, beg WS row, shape edges of circle as foll:

**Next 6 rows:** Dec 1 from first edge of Medallion opening; bind off 2 from next edge of Medallion opening.

**Next 4 rows:** Dec 1 from first edge; dec 1 from next edge.

Dec 1 st from each edge every other row 4 times, every 3rd row twice, every 4th row once—a total of 20 sts decreased from each edge of opening.

Work 15 rows even.

**Next Row:** (RS) Cast on 1 st each edge.

Cont to cast on 1 st each edge every 4th row once, every 3rd row twice, EOR 4 times, every row 4 times.

**Next 5 rows (beg RS row):** On RS rows, cast on 2 sts at each edge; on WS rows, cast on 1 st each edge—a total of 20 sts increased each edge.

**Next Row:** (WS) Cast on 11 sts after first edge and cont to work WS row with same yarn to join top of circle.

AT SAME TIME, when piece measures 12½″ from beg, end with WS row; last buttonhole is ½″ below.

**Shape Front Neck:** (RS) Cont Medallion opening on Back sts, on Right Front [p1, k1] twice, p1, ssk; on Left

Front work to last 7 sts, k2tog, [p1, k1] twice, p1. Cont to dec in this manner EOR until a total of 18 decs have been made, then work even for rem of piece.

AT SAME TIME, when piece measures ½″ from beg of Front neck shaping (4 rows), end with WS row.

**Shape Armholes:** (RS) Work to 4 sts before side marker; join new ball of yarn, bind off 8 sts, work across Back sections (the circle will still be divided), work to 4 sts before side marker, join new ball of yarn, bind off 8 sts, work to end. Working each section with separate balls of yarn, work 1 row even. (Place sts for Back pieces on holder or cont to work all pieces at same time.)

(RS) At each armhole edge, dec 1 st EOR 8 times, working [k1, ssk] on right edge, [k2tog, k1] on left edge.

Cont to shape neck, work even at armhole edges until armhole measures 7½ (8, 8½, 9)″ from beg of shaping, end with WS row.

### SHOULDERS
Bind off all rem sts of Right Front; bind off Left Front to 5 Rib sts of Left band; do not bind off last 5 sts.

### BACK NECKBAND
Working on 5 sts of Left Front band, work even until piece measures 7″ from shoulder bind off. Bind off.

### BACK
(If you put the Back on holders, resume medallion, AT SAME TIME shape armholes as for Front.)

When armhole measures 7½ (8, 8½, 9)″ from beg of shaping, bind off rem sts.

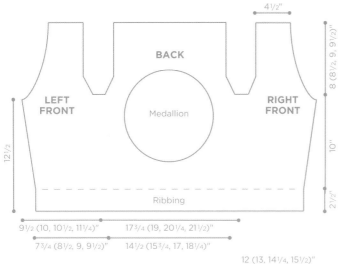

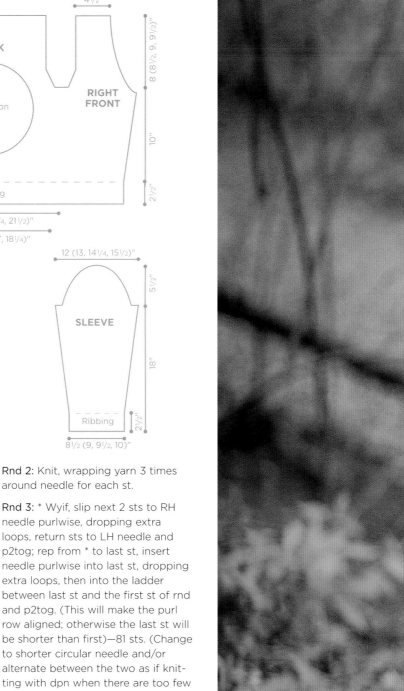

### SLEEVE

Using shorter needle and long-tail cast-on method, cast on 43 (45, 47, 49) sts; beg 1x1 Rib. Work even until piece measures 2½″ from beg, end with WS row. Beg St st.

**Small (Medium) only:** Work even until piece measures 4½″ from beg, end with WS row.

**All sizes:** (RS) Inc 1 st each side this row, then every 10 (10, 8, 8) rows 7 times, every 6th row 0 (2, 4, 6) times, working inc sts in St st—59 (65, 71, 77) sts.

Work even until piece measures 18″ from beg, end with WS row.

**Shape Sleeve Cap:** Bind off 4 sts at beg of next 2 rows, then dec 1 st each side EOR 8 times—35 (41, 47, 53) sts. Work even for 1″, then dec 1 st EOR 6 times, every row 6 times—11 (17, 23, 29) sts rem; bind off.

### FINISHING

Sew shoulder seams. Sew Back Neckband across Back neck; graft end of Back Neckband to bound off end of Right Front band. Sew sleeve seams; set in sleeves. Sew buttons opposite buttonholes.

### MEDALLION

With RS facing, pm at 12, 3, 6 and 9 o'clock around the opening in Back. Using longer circular needle, beg at lower edge to the LH side of initial bind off of 11 sts, pick up and knit 161 sts around circle—40 sts between each marker, plus 1 extra st.

Rnd 1: Purl.

Rnd 2: Knit, wrapping yarn 3 times around needle for each st.

Rnd 3: * Wyif, slip next 2 sts to RH needle purlwise, dropping extra loops, return sts to LH needle and p2tog; rep from * to last st, insert needle purlwise into last st, dropping extra loops, then into the ladder between last st and the first st of rnd and p2tog. (This will make the purl row aligned; otherwise the last st will be shorter than first)—81 sts. (Change to shorter circular needle and/or alternate between the two as if knitting with dpn when there are too few sts for comfort.)

Rnds 4 and 5: Rep Rnds 2 and 3 —41 sts.

Rnd 6: Knit, wrapping yarn 3 times around needle for each st.

Rnd 7: Purl, dropping extra loops.

Rnds 8-11: Rep Rnds 6 and 7 twice.

Rnds 12-15: Rep Rnds 2 and 3 twice —11 sts.

Bind off all sts purlwise.

# CHAPTER 2

# PLANES

*Adventures in Texture,
Stitch Patterns,
and Directional Construction*

LIKE THE COMPUTER, KNITTING WORKS ON A BINARY SYSTEM. FROM JUST two stitches, knit and purl (and a few manipulations), a whole world of textures is made. I find this magical and satisfying; the entire craft of knitting has evolved from two basic elements. The other manipulations and considerations of knitting seem to be organized in pairs as well—yarn overs and decreases, left and right slants, cables placed as mirror images. This symmetry makes sense to us. We've been trained to think and see in polarities: black and white, on and off, right and wrong. This perspective makes knitting comprehensible, but when we're inspired to think outside the box—about asymmetry, counterbalance, negative space—an exciting expanse of possibilities between the polarities, and maybe even beyond the margins, is revealed.

The designs in this chapter reflect the dualities in knitting and in life. Their vocabulary is that of traditional stitchwork (ribs, cables, eyelet lace) often used in nontraditional ways. When we view an object we instinctively look for the places where elements reflect or repeat and where they diverge. Here, I wanted to create visual tension between opposite forces—the juxtaposition of flat with raised, angled with straight, symmetry with asymmetry, soft with hard, romantic with edgy, ancient with modern.

Reviewing the collection, I realize it shows a recurring use of triangular shapes, both in stitch motif and styling, which attempts, literally, to bridge the polarities: two opposite ends angle inward to conjoin. The woven and braided patterns used throughout are another visual metaphor for the intersecting of opposites. In those designs, the planes of two adjacent sides, actually (or appear to) overlap each other.

In addition, it is often the proportions and curves of the body that inform the construction and pattern placement. Our bodies, like many things in nature, are bilaterally symmetrical, and the female form has the added vertical symmetry of the hip and bust "hourglass." However, no two sides are truly equal—gather leaves on an autumn day and see what remarkable variations on a theme nature provides. Nature doesn't replicate like a computer. And, in fact, our internal organs are not bilaterally symmetrical. We each have one, albeit complex, heart. Often I find myself, whether subconsciously or not, giving emphasis to the left side of the sweater front. It is as if the flow of the design is pulled to the site of the heart, the vital place that culturally is seen as the core of our feelings.

## corrugated asymmetrical v-neck and hat

I love browsing in stationery and art supply stores. The fantastic materials—paper pressed with everything from petals to feathers to gold leaf, jellylike vellums, elaborate, gauzy cutwork—make me wish for a life of clever dinner parties and custom-made thank-you notes. One of the novelties I'm most drawn to is a refined version of cardboard made with the ripples exposed rather than sandwiched within. The texture of corrugated stripes, resembling a washboard or shutters, is rustic, but it also reminds me of modern sculpture. It motivated me to create this stitch pattern. The purl ridges in the garter stitch are separated by knit-stitch hinges and lie flat; the reverse-stockinette bands puff up to create waves in the fabric. Make the hat (shown on page 21) first and use it as your gauge swatch for the sweater.

>> *See pattern on page 84.*

## slinky tree bark rib tunic

Joseph Campbell wrote, "God is the experience of looking at a tree and saying 'Ah.'" There is a very old tree in the lot behind my apartment building. It obscures the panorama of fire escapes out my back window, rising above the six-story structures. After rainstorms, I open the sash and breathe in beneficial negative ions from its dark branches, swaying over my roof. The tree's furrowed bark inspired my yarn choice for this design—slick yet spongy gray—and the stitch pattern. Small traveling ribs offer organic movement within the tall, fluted column of the sweater. The tunic silhouette, which I use as the basis of many of my designs, is borrowed from a fifteenth-century undershirt.

>> See pattern on page 88.

## irregular rib raglan with toggle

Why are rib patterns so regimented (2x2, 4x4, etc.) and not varied for interesting vertical striping? It's probably because unless a pattern is repetitive, a knitter's rhythm is broken (or never established), necessitating the counting of knits and purls. When we memorize a repeat, our hands work the next stitch seemingly without command.

Would an irregular rib deny this blissful aspect of knitting? It needn't. Pianists memorize entire pieces with complicated rhythms, fingerings, and keys. How many numbers are stored in our memory already—telephone, Social Security, PIN? The challenge is to memorize an eight-digit rib sequence like a phone number. Once you get the sequence in your mind, let your fingers "speed dial."

>> See pattern on page 90.

## diagonal twist princess-seam jacket

Princess seams are a tailoring solution for the hourglass figure; the fitted segments of the bodice draw in and let out fabric along the torso's vertical lines for a better fit. I have done a handknit version of the technique here.

This jacket reminds me of black-and-white Tudor architecture, in which the exposed timber-frame supports, blackened with tar, are set off by white "wattle and daub" plaster, segmenting the structure with vertical, and often opposing diagonal, lines. I love the concept of exposing the "bones," so to speak, for decorative effects. So I've borrowed this idea of emphasizing a segmented structural solution. Rather than contrast of color and material, I've used textural and directional stitchwork to set off the segments. The tweedy yarn lends a stucco-like surface.

*>> See pattern on page 92.*

### ragamuffin pullover and earflap hat

I love shabby-chic fashion that is distressed on purpose. It imitates the bohemian idyll of the SoHo I knew as a teenager when struggling artists lived there, before it became New York City's touristy shopping strip. Now, I like to dress my daughter as a little ragamuffin. When she receives the inevitable Gap cardigan or Old Navy fleece, I embroider it or add patches and mix it with thrift-shop finds, layering the colorful with the drab, weaving the old with the new.

I based this ensemble upon an imagined fable of a resourceful mother who used odd scraps of yarn to darn a threadbare piece or extended the main color of a knitted garment with a motley assortment of leftovers. It also illustrates two ways to create a braided or woven pattern: The pullover embodies the ersatz way, with small woven motifs similar to the ends of the Braided Neckpiece (page 118), while the pattern of the Earflap Hat (shown on page 96) is worked with real braided cables.

>> See pattern on page 96.

## unisex basketweave v-neck and scarf

The year I worked for *Vogue Knitting*, my coworkers and I decided to knit scarves for each other for holiday gifts, all in an easy basketweave stitch. Each staff member drew the name of another, then we circulated shade card books to pick yarn for our secret knitter to use.

I chose a straw yellow—exactly the shade I've chosen for this sweater. Among the sixty other colors in the binder, this one spoke to me. While knitting Rosemary's scarf in vibrant royal blue, I sometimes doubted my choice—all those colors and I pick a piss yellow beige! But when my scarf arrived, knit in Charlotte's even stitchwork, I found it to be soothing to the eye and utilitarian, a lovely golden basket.

To complement the sweater here, I've called upon the basketweave scarf again, but this time I've colored in the purl blocks. For fun, I've let the yarn ends hang out as an all-over fringe. I've chosen colors reminiscent of the 1970s, colors that predate digital color printing, earthen and burnished but with an inky, silkscreen flavor.

>> *See pattern on page 100.*

## braided-bodice wench blouse

With this design, I wanted to echo the phony "braided cable" I used in the Braided Neckpiece (page 118), but with real Aran stitchwork. When I saw how the braided cable puckered my chenille swatch like smocked velvet, my Goth tendencies took over, and I went full-out with costumey, puffy sleeves.

I'm baffled by the Goth influences that sometimes manifest on my knitting needles. I'm not into Anne Rice's vampire chronicles, I left Bilbo in some grotto halfway through *The Hobbit*, and I can't say I'd feel at home in the Goth subculture: a darkly poetic, somewhat occult offshoot of the punk rock movement of the '80s. But Goth is lightening up these days: A visit to www.gothfashion.info offers glitter Goths, industrial Goths, tribal Goths, and spaghetti western Goths. There's even a Renaissance Festival–inspired feminist movement called WENCH, or "Women Entitled to Nothing but Complete Happiness." That is something to wish for as you knit—and wear—this top.

>> See pattern on page 102.

## yarn-over steek vest

When I was a teenager, my mother arranged for me to study with a disciple of Alvin Nicolais, who developed a form of modern dance based on contact improvisation. I always feared the last minutes of the class, when we had to improvise movements upon command—your brain is located in your knee; your left side is full of lead and your right side is full of feathers; you breathe through your navel—and solo across the floor. Now, I'm thankful I was pushed to translate extreme concepts into a physical medium—it makes me a more daring designer—but glad there's no video replay.

The dropped-stitch panel across the front of this vest was inspired by the illustration of a wound steek in Alice Starmore's *Book of Fair Isle Knitting*. In this method of creating an opening in a knitted piece, a series of yarn overs creates a span of working yarn that later can be cut, sewn, and hidden. Why not put a wound steek up the front of a vest, I wondered, and leave the yarn running across? The resulting vest has a hole up the front (sounds like one of my dance exercises), and each strand of yarn has its solo across the chest.

>> See pattern on page 104.

## cashmere lace blouse

I wanted a lacy stitch for this top, one that was delicate but geometric to echo the deep angled ribbing. I came across a very old stitch pattern called English Mesh Lace. It resembles metal filigree with its trellis-like grid, the lines of which appear to alternately recede and advance, with a leafy filler inside the diamonds of the grid. Working the pattern felt to me like a little dance of my hands. I searched the Internet (www.streetswing.com has an index of dance history) to find just what dance paralleled the small, repetitive swinging movements needed to form the peaked decreases on alternate sets of stitches. It was the minuet—a slow, stately dance in which you arch up on the right foot, close the heels together, and plié, then arch up on the left foot, close the heels, and plié. With this rhythm in my mind and in my fingers, I put on a CD of Keith Jarrett playing harpsichord and got into the groove.

>> See pattern on page 106.

## lace leaf pullover

The loop-d-loop Leaf Cravat that I refined for *Interweave Knits*, Winter 2002/2003, was a popular project among knit bloggers—computer-savvy knitters who routinely post "Web logs" and pictures of projects on the Internet—and I enjoyed spotting their photos while browsing. The scarf design was jewelry-influenced. A coiled bracelet with snake heads at the ends gave me the idea for a less venomous form for my knitted "necklace." For its next incarnation, I thought it would be nice to extend the scarf into a sweater, to place a motif at the neck as if the scarf's leaf ends were tied there. I repeated the motif at the hem and on one cuff, aiming for a '50s gamine but curvy silhouette.

>> See pattern on page 110.

## braided neckpiece

A few winters ago, Banana Republic featured a keyhole scarf—a clever cravat with one end secured through a hole on the other end—and patterns for them started cropping up in knitting magazines. This gave me an idea: What would happen if I made more than one hole and then multiple straps at the other side? I found I could weave the two sides together, mimicking the braided cable or entrelac. Making this type of scarf is as fun as the potholders we made in grade school by weaving nylon loops on a frame—but the result is much more sophisticated, especially in ivory cashmere.

>> *See pattern on page 118.*

## asymmetrical mock cable vest/pullover and hat

Since the beginning of the Aran sweater, knitters have improvised their own arrangement of motifs to fill a sweater body. For this avant-garde design (a favorite on my website), I abstracted a giant cable to appear an organic part of the sweater's form by crossing at the V of the neck. To avoid the bulk of a standard cable twist, I used a mock cable technique, filling in the cable and half of the back with one of my favorite Aran textures, Irish Moss. It's named for the algae (carrageenan) plentiful on Ireland's coasts, which is used as a natural "filler" in everything from toothpaste to ice cream (and here, an Aran cable).

>> *See pattern on page 112.*

## cabled riding jacket

The texture of wool stitchwork has a particularly Romantic quality, as does the story of this jacket's beginnings. A photographer once approached me with a scruffy, ribbed gansey in authentically oily navy blue wool, a gift from his mentor, photographer George Platt Lynes. "This is the sweater that transformed my life," he told me, and wondered if I could resurrect or replicate it. A slight, unathletic man with low confidence, he found that when he donned the gansey, his shoulders seemed more virile, his complexion more rugged. It made him feel like a Greek god. He wore this sweater whenever he presented himself at agencies, and doors opened.

I set out to create the feminine equivalent of that transforming sweater. I filled an hourglass silhouette by experimenting with cables—shifting their direction, twisting them more frequently, shaping between them, and putting them on the bias. I sought a wool yarn of an authentic, artisinal quality, one that was soft but had enough body to show off the cables and give the jacket structure. I found it in Margaret Klein Wilson's "Mostly Merino," spun from her own flock in Vermont by a local mill, Green Mountain Spinnery, and dyed by herself in small batches. Whether your medium is fiber or photography, this is a garment for the artist in you.

*>> See pattern on page 120.*

# corrugated asymmetrical
# v-neck and hat

## OVERVIEW

This sweater is worked straight on a circular needle to accommodate the width of Piece 1 and because the flexibility of a circular needle is required for picking up sleeve sts from underarm.

You will make two garment pieces (see diagrams on page 86). The first is shaped like an upside-down T; its cast on edge spans the length of the sweater from Front hem to Back hem, with the Sleeve extending from center. You'll bind off at each edge for the side seam, then cont to the cuff. The second piece also has a Sleeve sandwiched between Front and Back. You'll begin at the neck edge and work on the bias (at roughly a 45-degree angle to the other piece), by increasing at each edge until there is enough width for the sleeve and body. You'll then put the sleeve stitches on hold and work even on the body stitches on-the-bias, by making decreases at the center of the row (side seam) to compensate for the edge increases. When no more length is needed to match to Piece 1, after leaving space for the neck drop, you will get rid of stitches by binding off at the beg of every row—the edges now become the lower hem and your bind offs eventually meet at the side seam.

## SIZES

**hat (see pages 21 and 92):**
One size fits Child's 5 and older to Woman's Small/Medium

20" circumference

**v-neck:**
<Child's 2T–4T (5–7 years, 8–10 years)>;

Woman's Small (Medium, Large)

**Shown in <2T–4T>; Small.**

## KNITTED MEASUREMENTS

**Chest:** <25 (27, 29)">; 32 (37, 40)"

**Length:** <13 (15, 17)">; 21 (22, 23)"

**Sleeve width at upper arm:** <10 (11, 12)">; 12¾ (14, 15¼)"

## YARN

Goddess Yarns "Jay" (70% wool/30% alpaca), 2-ply bulky

<4 (5, 6) balls (3.5oz/ 100g; 87yd/80m) in 5084 red>; 8 (9, 11) balls in B118 brown

1 ball for gauge swatch hat

## NEEDLES/TOOLS

US 10½ (6.5mm) <24" long circular>; 32" long, or size to match gauge

US 10½ (6.5mm) any length circular (for holding Piece 2 sleeve sts and helping to work first few sleeve rows)

Stitch markers

Tapestry needle

Straight pins

## GAUGE

12 sts and 18 rows = 4" in Stitch pattern (knitting Hat is a great way to test gauge)

3 rows = 1" in Stitch pattern, when bound off on bias

I prefer not to block this garment, so that it retains the rippled, corrugated effect. To measure gauge, lay piece on even surface and press down flat with ruler.

Always check and MATCH gauge for best fit.

## STITCH PATTERN

Also see Corrugated Chart.

**Row 1:** (RS) Knit—Garter st (knit every row).

**Rows 2–6:** Cont in Garter st.

**Rows 7–10:** Work in St st (knit on RS rows; purl on WS rows).

**Rows 11–14:** Work in Rev St st (purl on RS rows; knit on WS rows).

**Rows 15–18:** Work in St st.

Rep Rows 1–18 for St patt.

## hat

Using long-tail cast-on method, cast on 60 sts; beg St st. (WS) Work even for 7 rows. (RS) Change to St patt; work even until piece measures 5″ from beg, end with a WS row.

**Shape Top of Hat:** (RS) Work left-slanting dec (ssk if a knit row or p2tog if a purl row), work 26 sts, work right-slanting dec (k2tog if a knit row or p2tog-tbl if a purl row), place marker (pm), left-slanting dec, work to last 2 sts, right-slanting dec; 4 decs made, one at each edge and

**CORRUGATED CHART**

**KEY**

☐ Knit on RS, purl on WS.

⊟ Purl on RS, knit on WS.

2 in center of row (which becomes the other side seam of hat)—56 sts.

Work 1 row even.

**Next Row:** Dec, work to 2 sts before marker, dec, slip marker (sl m), dec, work to last 2 sts, dec. Cont to dec in this manner EOR until 32 sts rem; bind off all sts. Using tapestry needle and yarn, sew side seam and top of hat closed.

## v-neck
### PIECE 1
### (Right half of sweater—Front, Back, and Sleeve)

Using long-tail cast-on method, cast on <80 (90, 102)>; 126 (132, 138) sts. Tie (and leave) a yarn marker at center of cast on row, to mark for assembling pieces—this is top right shoulder. (WS) Beg St patt with Row 2 (the cast on row counts as Row 1 of first rep); work Rows 3–18, then Rep Rows 1–18 until piece measures <4 (4¼, 4½)″>; 4 (4½, 5)″.

<Skip shaping and proceed to * below.>

### Shape Armhole and Shoulder (Woman's sizes only):

**Row 1:** Work 45 (46, 47), pm, inc (k-f/b), work 34 (38, 42), inc, work to end—128 (134, 140) sts.

**Row 2 and all WS rows:** Work even.

**Row 3:** Work to marker, inc, work 36 (40, 44), inc, work to end—130 (136, 142) sts.

**Rows 5 and 7:** Work to marker, inc, work 17 (19, 21), dec (left-slanting—ssk if a knit row or p2tog if a purl row), dec (right-slanting—k2tog if a knit row or p2tog-tbl if a purl row), k17 (19, 21), inc, work to end—130 (136, 142) sts.

**Row 8:** Rep Row 2.

*Right Side Seam

(RS) Bind off <25 (28, 33)>; 46 (47, 48) sts at beg next 2 rows—<30 (34, 36)>; 38 (42, 46) sts.

## SLEEVE

Cont in patt on these <30 (34, 36)>; 38 (42, 46) sts, dec 1 st each side every <8th>; 10th row <4>; 5 (6, 7) times—<22 (26, 28)>; 28 (30, 32) sts. Work even until sleeve measures <9 (11, 13)″>; 18″, or desired length, ending with the closest full rep of either Garter st or Rev St st. *Note: Because sleeve is knit from top down you can always adjust the length—especially as children's arm lengths vary: Drape the piece over the intended wearer, pin the side seams together, and find the best length.* Bind off all sts loosely. Fold piece in half from cast on marker along center length of Sleeve (right of marker is Back, left is Front) and sew side and sleeve seam.

## PIECE 2
### (Left half of sweater—Front, Back, and Sleeve)

Using long-tail cast-on method, cast on <36 (40, 44)>; 56 (58, 60) sts. Tie (and leave) a yarn marker at center of cast on row to mark for assembling pieces—this is top left shoulder. (WS) Beg St patt with Row 2 (the cast on row counts as Row 1 of first rep); work Rows 3–8, then Rep Rows 1–18; AT SAME TIME, shape each end as follows:

**Row 1:** (WS) Knit.

**Row 2:** Inc, work across to last 2 sts, inc, k1 (selvedge stitch for cleaner edge).

Cont as est, inc 1 st each end EOR (at beg and end of each RS row) <14 (16, 18)>; 19 (23, 26) times total—<64 (72, 80)>; 94 (104, 112) sts. You will cont to increase at each end as est, but now piece measures <6¼ (7¼, 8)″>; 8¼ (10¼, 11½)″.

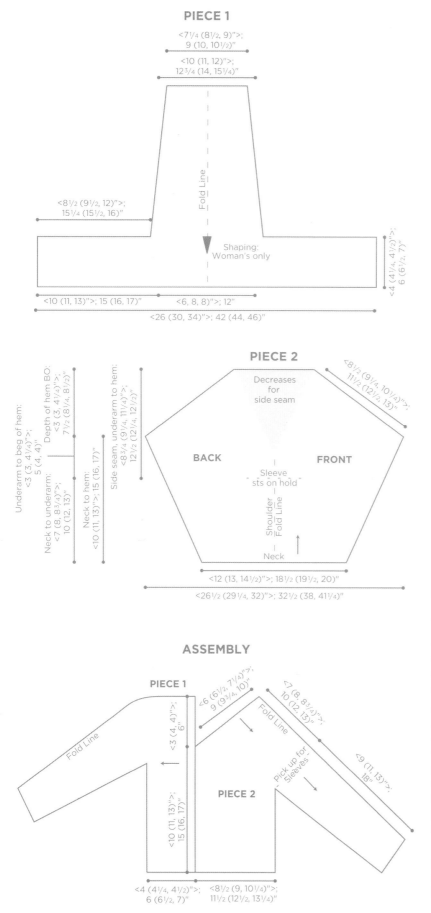

**PIECE 1**

<7¼ (8½, 9)">;
9 (10, 10½)"

<10 (11, 12)">;
12¾ (14, 15¼)"

Fold Line

Shaping:
Woman's only

<8½ (9½, 12)">;
15¼ (15½, 16)"

<4 (4¼, 4½)">;
6 (6½, 7)"

<10 (11, 13)">; 15 (16, 17)"        <6, 8, 8)">; 12"

<26 (30, 34)">; 42 (44, 46)"

**PIECE 2**

Decreases
for
side seam

<8½ (9¼, 10¼)">;
11½ (12½, 13)"

BACK            FRONT

Sleeve
sts on hold

Shoulder
Fold Line

Neck

Underarm to beg of hem:
<3 (3, 4¼)">;
5 (4, 4)"

Depth of hem BO:
<3 (3, 4¼)">;
7½ (8¼, 8½)"

Neck to underarm:
<7 (8, 8¾)">;
10 (12, 13)"

Neck to hem:
<10 (11, 13)">; 15 (16, 17)"

Side seam, underarm to hem:
<8¾ (9¼, 11¼)">;
12½ (12¼, 12½)"

<12 (13, 14½)">; 18½ (19½, 20)"

<26½ (29¼, 32)">; 32½ (38, 41¼)"

**ASSEMBLY**

PIECE 1

Fold Line

<3 (4, 4)">;
6"

<6 (6½, 7¼)">;
9 (9¾, 10)"

Fold Line

<7 (8, 8¾)">;
10 (12, 13)"

Pick up for
Sleeves

PIECE 2

<9 (11, 13)">;
18"

<10 (11, 13)">;
15 (16, 17)"

<4 (4¼, 4½)">;
6 (6½, 7)"

<8½ (9, 10¼)">;
11½ (12½, 13¼)"

**Shape Armhole:** (RS) Inc, work <19 (21, 24)>; 28 (31, 33), pm, inc, work <22 (26, 28)>; 34 (38, 42), inc, pm, work to last 2 sts, inc, k1—<68 (76, 84)>; 98 (108, 116) sts.

**Next and all WS rows:** Work even, sl m.

**Next RS row:** Inc, work across to marker, sl m, inc, work to 1 st before marker, sl m, inc, work to last 2 sts, inc, k1—<72 (80, 88)>; 102 (112, 120) sts.

<Cont to inc 4 sts across RS rows as est twice more—80 (88, 96) sts, work a WS row—piece measures 7 (8, 8¾)" from cast on; cont from Dividing Row below.>

**Shape Shoulder (Women's sizes only):** (RS) Inc, work across to marker, inc, work 17 (19, 21), dec (left slanting), dec (right slanting), k17 (19, 21), inc, work to last 2 sts, inc, k1—104 (114, 122) sts. Work 1 row even. Rep last 2 rows once—106 (116, 124) sts. Piece measures 10 (12, 13)" from cast on.

**Dividing Row:** (RS) Inc, work <24 (26, 29)>; 33 (36, 38), place next <30 (34, 36)>; 38 (42, 46) sts on spare circular needle for Sleeve (it is helpful to jot down which row St patt left off on), do not cut yarn—by skipping Sleeve sts and cont to work on the st after, you join sweater Front to Back; pm for side seam, work to last 2 sts, inc, k1—<52 (56, 62)>; 70 (76, 80) sts, [<26 (28, 31)>; 35 (38, 40), each Front and Back].

**BODY**

**Next and all WS rows (until hem):** Work even.

(RS) Inc, work to 2 sts before marker, dec (left-slanting), sl m, dec (right-slanting), work to last 2 sts, inc, k1— no change in stitch count.

Cont as est, working inc at each end and dec before and after marker for <3 (3, 4¼)">; 5 (4, 4)" more, so that the outer edge, which will be sewn at cast on to neck drop, measures approx <10 (11, 13)">; 15 (16, 17)" when slightly rippled (measure without pressing down on ruler so not completely flattened).

**HEM**

Cont in patt as est, discontinue the incs at beg and end of RS rows;

instead, beg to form bottom hem by binding off (loosely) the first st of every row; AT SAME TIME, cont to work dec at side seam before and after marker until 8 sts rem—this will get rid of 4 sts over every 2 rows, so should take approx <26 (28, 31)>; 35 (38, 40) rows.

**Next row:** (RS) Bind off 1, dec, dec, k2—5 sts.

**Next row:** Bind off 1, work to end.

**Next row:** Dec, dec, turn; bind off rem 2 sts. From center underarm to hem at left side seam, piece should measure <8 3/4 (9 1/4, 11 1/4)">; 12 3/4 (12 1/2, 12 3/4)". Cut yarn.

### SLEEVE

With RS facing, join yarn and cont with next patt row on <30 (34, 36)>; 38 (42, 46) Sleeve sts. Use the 2 circular needles until enough length at armhole seam to be comfortable with one needle; AT SAME TIME

**Shape Sleeve:** Dec 1 st each side every <8th>; 10th row <4>; 5 (6, 7) times—<22 (26, 28)>; 28 (30, 32) sts.

Work even until sleeve measures <9 (11, 13)">; 18", or desired length, ending with the closest full rep of either Garter stitch or Rev St st.

*Note: The left Sleeve can be a bit shorter than the right Sleeve to compensate for the looser drape over the shoulder and to end on a row in patt rep that more closely matches other cuff—try the piece on intended wearer before binding off.*

Fold sleeve in half lengthwise and sew seam.

### FINISHING

Match pieces together to pin Front and Back seams as per assembly diagram at left: Match cast on edge of Piece 1 to side edges of Piece 2, leaving <3 (4, 4)">; 6" for neck drop open at each side of Piece 1's cast on row marker; and match the outer edge of Piece 1 cast on row to the corner formed by first hem bind off row on Piece 2. To retain ripple effect, gather bias edge of Piece 2 a bit when pinning. Sew Front and Back seams. Weave in ends.

# slinky tree bark rib tunic

This tunic is worked in 2x2 Rib with a "Traveling Rib" motif created with simple increases and decreases strategically placed to skew the Rib. It is done in small marked areas and in rounds so you always see the front of the fabric. As you work the motif you will begin to internalize its "rules": There is one inc and one dec per row so number of sts is constant, the decs pull a column of knits to the left on the lower chart then to the right on the upper chart, and the increases unfold as Rib creating first 2 knits then 2 purls, so on Chart Rows 8 and 16 the 2x2 Rib is re-established. Once you get the hang of placing the motif, challenge yourself to individualize your version by placing the motif as you like on the sleeves.

## STITCH PATTERN
**Traveling Rib Motif** (see Chart)

## BODY
Using long-tail cast-on method, cast on 164 (180, 196) sts. Pm on RH needle for beg of round (left side seam). Join, being careful not to twist sts.

**Establish Pattern: Rnd 1:** [P2, k2] 20 (22, 24) times, p2, pm for right side seam, [p2, k2] 20 (22, 24) times, p2.

*Note: The 2x2 Rib is broken by 4 purl sts at each side seam.*

Cont as established (knit the knit sts and purl the purl sts), work even until piece measures 3" from beg.

**First Motifs:** *Work 46 (50, 54) sts as est, pm; beg Traveling Rib Motif (work Rnd 1 of Chart across next 18 sts), pm; work 18 (22, 26) sts as est, slip marker (sl m) for side seam; rep from * once.

Cont as est, working Motif between markers, until 16 rows of Motif are completed. Work even in Rib for 1".

**Second Motifs:** *Work 26 (30, 34) sts as est, pm; beg Motif, pm; work 38 (42, 46) sts as est, sl m; rep from * once.

Cont as for First Motifs, working even as est for 2" after completion of Motifs.

**Third Motifs:** *Work 34 (38, 42) sts as est, pm; beg Motif, pm; work 30 (34, 38) sts as est, sl m; rep from * once.

## SIZES
Small (Medium, Large)

*When choosing size consider how the fabric will be un-stretched (waist), slightly stretched or very stretched (hips/bust) over the figure.*

**Shown in Small.**

## KNITTED MEASUREMENTS
**Circumference of Body:** 27 (29½, 32)" unstretched; 32 (35, 38)" slightly stretched; 41 (45, 49)" very stretched

**Length:** 30½ (31, 31½)" when flat—loses about 3" length when stretched around body

**Sleeve at upper arm:** 14 (14¾, 16)" slightly stretched

## YARN
Berroco "Softwool" (59% viscose/41% wool), worsted, three 2-ply strands with 3 single-ply strands

11 (13, 15) hanks (1.75oz/50g; 100yd/92m) in 9475 gray granite

## NEEDLES/TOOLS
US 7 (4.5mm) 24" long circular, or size to match gauge

Stitch markers

Tapestry needle

## GAUGE
16 sts and 28 rows = 4" in 2x2 Rib very stretched

20 sts and 28 rows = 4" in 2x2 Rib slightly stretched

24 sts and 28 rows = 4" in 2x2 Rib unstretched

Always check and MATCH gauge for best fit.

Work as for Second Motifs.

**Fourth Motifs:** *Work 42 (46, 50) sts as est, pm; beg Motif, pm; work 22 (26, 30) sts as est, sl m; rep from * once.

Work as for Second Motifs.

**Fifth Motifs:** *Work 18 (24, 28) sts as est, pm; beg Motif, pm; work 46 (50, 54) sts as est, sl m; rep from * once.

When Motifs are completed, piece measures 22½" from beg.

**Divide for Front and Back:** * P2, k1, ssk, work as est to 5 sts before side marker, k2tog, k1, p2—80 (88, 96) sts for Front; discard marker, join a new ball of yarn and rep from * for Back. Place Front sts on holder.

### BACK

(WS) Working on Back sts only, work 1 row even as est.

**Shape Armholes:** (RS) * P2, k1, ssk, work as est to last 5 sts, k2tog, k1, p2. Work 1 row even.

Rep from * 2 times more, for a total of 4 dec rows—74 (82, 90) sts.

**Next Row:** (RS) Work 14 (18, 22) sts as est, pm; beg Motif, work Row 1 of Chart, pm; work 42 (46, 50) sts as est.

Work as for First Motifs, then work even as est until armhole measures 8 (8½, 9)" from Dividing Row. Bind off loosely in Rib (be careful not to bind off too tightly).

### TRAVELING RIB MOTIF

### KEY

**Circular:** Work all rows from right to left.
**Straight:** Work RS rows from right to left, WS rows from left to right.

☐ Knit on RS, purl on WS.

⊟ Purl on RS, knit on WS.

☑ Inc: K-f/b or p-f/b in pattern

◩ k2tog

◪ ssk

### FRONT

Work as for Back until armhole measures 4" from Dividing Row (about ¾" after Motifs are completed)—74 (82, 90) sts; pm between 2 center sts.

**Shape Neck Slit:** (RS) Work as est to center st (1 st before marker), p1; join a new ball of yarn, p1 (center st), work as est to end. Working both sides at same time with separate balls of yarn, work even until Front slit measures 3", end with a WS row.

**Shape Neck:** At each neck edge, bind off 18 (19, 20) sts (beg of RS row for right Front; beg of WS row for left Front)—19 (22, 25) sts each shoulder. Cont as established, work even until piece measures same as Back to shoulders (1 [1½, 2]" from neck bind off). Bind off rem sts loosely in rib.

Graft shoulder seams.

### RIGHT SLEEVE

*Note: Sleeves are worked straight on circular needle.*

With RS facing, beg at right Back armhole after slant created by the armhole decs, pick up and knit 62 (66, 74) sts along straight edge, end

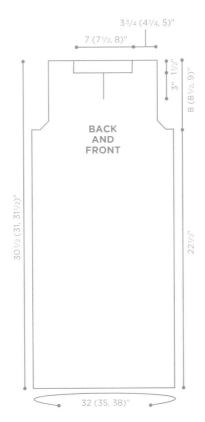

BACK AND FRONT

3¾ (4¼, 5)"
7 (7½, 8)"
3"  1½"
8 (8½, 9)"
30½ (31, 31½)"
22½"
32 (35, 38)"

at shaping on Front armhole (this is in a ratio of 2 sts per 3 rows so work into 2 rows then skip the next).

**Establish Pattern:** (WS) *P2, k2; rep from * to last 2 sts, p2 for 2x2 Rib.

**Shape Sleeve Cap:** Cont as est, inc 1 st each side every other row 4 times, working new sts in Rib—70 (74, 82) sts.

Work even as est for 2", end with a WS row.

**Shape Sleeve and place Motifs:** (RS) Dec 1 st each side every 10th (10th, 8th) row 10 (11, 14) times, placing motifs as desired—50 (52, 54) sts. (On RS rows, work as est in Rib, ending with p2 with at least 18 sts rem, pm; work Row 1 of Chart, pm; work as est to end. Complete motif as for Back and Front. On this sleeve I placed the motif 10" from top, toward the front). Work even until Sleeve measures 20" from beg, or desired length; bind off rem sts loosely in Rib.

### LEFT SLEEVE

Work as for right Sleeve, beg at left Front armhole, working along straight edge to Back. Place motif as desired. (On this sleeve I placed the motif centered 4" from bind off edge.)

### FINISHING

Sew sleeve seams and sew sleeve cap to armhole decs at underarm. Weave in ends.

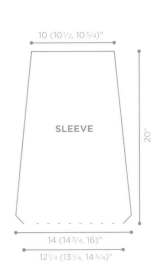

10 (10½, 10¾)"

SLEEVE

20"

14 (14¾, 16)"
12¼ (13¼, 14¾)"

# irregular rib raglan with toggle

## OVERVIEW

This sweater is knit in-the-round to the armholes, which are asymmetrical. The right armhole is shaped to accommodate a simple drop shoulder sleeve, while the left side has a raglan placket to match a raglan sleeve; the right side has a shoulder seam, whereas at the left side, the Back, Front, and Sleeve extend up to the Collar. To memorize the Irregular Rib pattern, think of it as a telephone number, keeping in mind that you will alternate between knit and purl: Say to yourself, "33122344-33122344-33122344."

## IRREGULAR RIB
(multiple of 22 sts)

**Row/Rnd 1:** (RS) *K3, p3, k1, p2, k2, p3, k4, p4; rep from * across/around.

**Row 2:** Knit the knit sts and purl the purl sts as they face you.

Rep Row 2 for Irregular Rib.

## BODY
Cast on 220 sts. Pm on RH needle for beg of round. Join, being careful not to twist sts. Beg Irregular Rib (10 reps per rnd); work even until piece measures 15" from the beg.

**Dividing Rnd/Row:** (RS) Bind off 3 sts; work in patt as est until 107 sts on RH needle after bind off for Front (1 st left from bind off, plus 106 worked); place rem sts on spare needle for Back.

## FRONT
(WS) Bind off 3 sts, work in patt as est to end; using single cast-on method, cast on 7 sts at end of row.

**Shape Armholes:** (RS) K2, p2, k3 over new sts, dec (left-slanting, use p2tog if st to the left is a purl st, use ssk if a knit st), work in patt as est to last 5 sts, dec (right-slanting, use p2tog-tbl if st to the right is a purl st, use k2tog if a knit st), work in patt to end. Work 1 row even. Rep these 2 rows, 3 times more—103 sts.

**Shape Raglan:** (RS) Decrease Row—K2, p2, k3, dec (left-slanting), work as est to end. Work 1 row even. Cont as est, at Raglan armhole only (beg of RS rows), dec 1 st EOR 25 more

## SIZE
One size fits small woman (sloppy "boyfriend sweater") to large man (fits up to 46" chest)

### KNITTED MEASUREMENTS
Chest: 48½"
Length: 27"
Sleeve at upper arm: 20"

## YARN
Rowan "Kid Classic" (70% lambswool/26% kid mohair/4% nylon), worsted weight, 3 singles with 2-ply strand

9 balls (1.75/50g; 151yd/140m) in 831 smoke

### NEEDLES/TOOLS
US 8 (5mm) 32" long circular for body, or size to match gauge

US 8 (5mm) 16" long circular for sleeves

## NOTIONS
Toggle button with leather base (see Resources)
Sharp "leather" sewing needle
Button thread

## GAUGE
18 sts and 24 rows = 4" in Irregular Rib, slightly stretched

Always check and MATCH gauge for best fit.

times—30 sts total have been decreased at raglan edge, after underarm bind off; armhole measures 10" from beg of shaping—77 sts.

### Shape Neck and Right Shoulder:
(The one the right arm will be in—it appears on the left from RS of fabric.)

(WS) Bind off 5 sts, work in patt as est until 35 sts on RH needle—37 sts rem; dec (right slanting), turn; place rem 35 sts at LH side (raglan edge) on holder for neck. (RS) Dec (left-slanting), work to end.

### Shape Shoulder:
(WS) At shoulder edge, bind off 5 sts; work to last 2 sts, dec (right slanting) at neck edge—28 sts.

Cont in this manner; bind off 5 sts at shoulder edge EOR (beg of WS rows) 4 times more for a total of 6 times, and AT SAME TIME, at neck edge, dec 1 st every row 8 times more, for a total of 12 times.

### BACK
With RS facing, join yarn to left underarm, bind off 3 sts, work as est to end.

(WS) Bind off 3 sts, work as est to end.

**Shape Armholes:** Work 3 sts as est, dec (left-slanting), work as est to last 5 sts, dec (right-slanting), work in patt to end. Work 1 row even. Rep these 2 rows 3 times more—96 sts. Work even for 2 rows, end with a WS row.

**Shape Raglan:** (RS) Decrease Row—Work as est to last 5 sts, dec (right-slanting), work in patt to end. Work 1 row even. Cont as est, at Raglan armhole only (end of RS rows), dec 1 st every 4th row 12 more times for a total of 13 times—83 sts. When

straight armhole measures 10" from beg of shaping,

Shape Right Shoulder as for Front, and AT SAME TIME, cont to dec at raglan edge every 4th row 3 more times—50 sts. Place rem sts on holder for neck.

### RIGHT SLEEVE—SET-IN
Cast on 50 sts. Pm on RH needle for beg of round. Join, being careful not to twist sts; beg Irregular Rib.

**Establish Pattern:** Working in-the-round, work 22-st rep twice, k3, p3. Cont as est, work 3 rows even.

**Shape Sleeve:** (RS) Inc 1 st at end of this rnd, then every 4th rnd 7 times, EOR 30 times, working new sts in patt as they become established (fill out partial rep at end of rnd, then begin patt rep again—this way you don't have to figure out how to work new sts in patt at beg of rnd)—88 sts. Work even until sleeve measures 18" from beg.

**Shape Cap:** (RS) Work to 3 sts before marker, bind of 6 sts, work to end—82 sts; beg working in rows. (WS) Work 1 row even.

**Next Row:** (RS) Work 3 sts in patt as est, dec (left-slanting), work as est to last 5 sts, dec (right-slanting), work in patt to end. Work 1 row even. Rep these 2 rows 3 times more—74 sts. Bind off all sts.

### LEFT SLEEVE—RAGLAN
Work as for right Sleeve until sleeve measures 18" from beg.

**Shape Raglan Armhole:** (RS) Work to 3 sts before marker, bind off 6 sts, work to end; cast on 7 sts at end of (RS) row. Beg working in rows.

**Establish Pattern:** (WS) Work new sts as K2, p2, k3, work in patt to end—89 sts.

(RS) Work 3 sts in patt as est, dec (left-slanting), work as est to last 9 sts, dec (right-slanting), work rem 7 sts p3, k2, p2. Work 1 row even. Rep these 2 rows 3 times more—81 sts.

(RS) Cont as est, shape the left edge of Raglan as for Front chest (dec 1 st EOR 26 more times), and right edge as for Back (dec 1 st every 4th row 16 times)—39 sts. Work until piece measures same as Back to neck; place rem sts on holder.

### FINISHING
Sew right shoulder seam. Set in right Sleeve. Sew left Sleeve to raglan on sweater Back; overlap the 7 cast-on sts at base of Front and Sleeve raglan, with Front piece on top. Using yarn and tapestry needle, topstitch along the 5th st in from edge (middle of purl stitch ridge) from armhole toward neck for 7". Weave in ends.

### COLLAR
With RS facing, beg at left Front neck edge (Raglan), work across 35 sts on neck holder in patt, pick up and knit 9 sts along Front neck shaping (you will work these in Irregular Rib, cont from chest sts; adjust patt as necessary); work in patt as est across 50 sts on Back neck holder, work across 39 sts at top of left Sleeve—133 sts. Work even in Irregular Rib until Collar measures 2½" from pick up row; bind off all sts loosely in patt.

### TOGGLE BUTTON
Sew toggle 3" below top edge of Collar. If you've purchased a toggle with a real leather base that does not come pre-punched with holes to guide sewing, use a sharp needle meant for leather to make an even number of small equidistant holes; place on sweater. Using strong button thread, sew to sweater with running stitch.

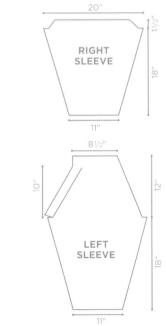
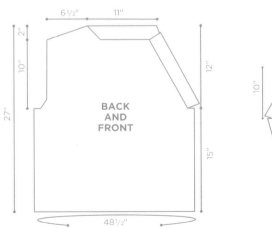

# diagonal twist princess-seam jacket

## OVERVIEW

This garment has an hourglass shape with about 9" differential from waist to chest. The jacket hem is worked from side to side, then bodice stitches are picked up and worked from the waist up—composed of 8 equal body segments bordered by 9 "spines" created by slipping and wrapping a column of stitches. The sleeves are picked up from the cuff in similar manner, with the center "spine" continuing across top of shoulder. The stitch pattern is raised, directional, and somewhat bulky, so for neatest results, when picking up or grafting stitches, it is necessary to closely observe how the upper sts cross over the lower and which stitch/row is next in line. When working the slip-wrap spines, do not pull yarn too tightly—let the wrapped sts retain their full width.

## STITCH PATTERNS
### 3-st Slip-wrap

Row 1: (WS) Purl.

Row 2: Wyif, sl 3 sts purlwise from LH needle to RH needle, yb, return 3 sts to LH needle without changing orientation, k3.

Rep Rows 1 and 2 for Slip-wrap.

### SIZES
X-Small (Small, Medium, Large)
**Shown in Small.**

### KNITTED MEASUREMENTS
**Chest:** 37 (39½, 41½, 44½)" closed

**Waist:** 27½ (30, 33, 35½)" closed

**Length:** 21½ (22, 22½, 23)"

### YARN
Classic Elite "Gatsby" (70% wool/15% viscose/15% nylon), bulky singles

8 (9, 10, 11) hanks (3.5oz/100g; 94yd/87m) in 2145 gold tweed

### NEEDLES/TOOLS
US 10½ (6.5mm) 32" or 36" long circular, or size to match gauge

Stitch markers

Stitch holders/spare circular needles

Tapestry needle

### NOTIONS
15 (15½, 16, 16½)" separating zipper

Sewing needle and matching thread

### GAUGE
12 sts and 16 rows = 4" over Diagonal Twist Rib

*Note: The left twist tends to be slightly looser than the right twist; swatch both, striving for even tension.*

Always check and MATCH gauge for best fit.

**Left Diagonal Twist Rib [L-Twist]:** see Chart on page 95.

**Right Diagonal Twist Rib [R-Twist]:** see Chart on page 95.

### HEM

Worked side-to-side, from right Front to left Front.

Using long-tail cast-on method, cast on 11 sts.

**Establish Pattern—Right Front:** (WS) Working Row 1 of each patt, work 3 sts in Slip-wrap, 8 sts in L-Twist.

Cont in patt as est until piece measures 6 (6¾, 7½, 8)″ from the beg, end with a RS row; pm (tie contrast yarn to beg of RS row) for side seam.

**Shape Right Hip:** Work Short Row Shaping as foll:

**Short Row Shaping**

*Change to 1x1 Rib over Twist sts.

**Short Row 1:** (WS) Cont Slip-wrap as est over first 3 sts, [p1, k1] 3 times, wrap next st, turn (wrp-t); (RS) [P1, k1] 3 times, work last 3 sts as est, turn.

**Short Row 2:** (WS) Work 3 sts as est, [p1, k1] 2 times, wrp-t; (RS) [p1, k1] 2 times, work to end, turn.

**Short Row 3:** (WS) Work 3 sts as est, p1, k1, wrp-t; (RS) P1, k1, work to end.

(WS) Work across all sts as est (p3, [p1, k1] 4 times), working wrap tog with wrapped st as you come to them.*

**Establish Pattern—Right Back:** (RS) Work Row 2 of R-Twist over 8 sts, work to end as est.

Cont as est, work even until shorter edge of piece measures 12¾ (14¼, 15¾, 16¾)″ from beg, end with (RS) Row 2 of patt; pm for center Back.

**Shape Center Back:** (WS) Rep Short Row Shaping, working from * to *.

**Establish Pattern—Left Back:** (RS) Work Row 2 of L-Twist over 8 sts, work to end as est.

Cont as est, work even until shorter edge of piece measures 6¾ (7½, 8¼, 8¾)″ from center Back marker, end with (RS) Row 2 of patt; pm for side seam.

**Shape Left Hip:** (WS) Rep Short Row Shaping, working from * to *.

**Establish Pattern—Left Front:** (RS) Work Row 2 of R-Twist over 8 sts, work to end as est.

Cont as est, work even until shorter edge of piece measures 25½ (28½, 31½, 33½)″—6 (6¾, 7½, 8)″ from side seam marker, end with a WS row.

### LEFT FRONT BAND

(RS) Bind off 7 sts, work to end as est—4 sts.

**Establish Pattern:** (WS) Work 3 sts as est, k1 (selvedge st).

Cont as est, work even until Slip-wrap "spine" measures same as bound off edge; bind off selvedge st, leave rem 3 sts on holder. Invisibly sew "spine" to bound off edge.

### RIGHT FRONT BAND

With RS facing, beg at right Front cast on edge, pick up and knit 3 sts in Slip-wrap sts, plus 1 st (selvedge st)—4 sts. Work as for Left Front Band, working first (WS) row: K1, work 3 sts in Slip-wrap.

### BODICE

*Note: It may be helpful to place additional markers at the halfway points between spine and side seam to pick up evenly across; pick up ratio is 3 sts for every 4 rows.*

With RS facing, working along shorter edge, beg right Front, work Slip-wrap over 3 sts from holder, evenly pick up and knit 18 (20, 22, 24) sts to side marker, 1 st at side seam, 19 (21, 23, 25) sts to center back marker, 1 st at center back, 19 (21, 23, 25) sts to side marker, 1 st at side seam, 18 (20, 22, 24) sts to the 3 sts on holder at left Front, work Slip-wrap over 3 sts from holder—83 (91, 99, 107) sts.

**Establish Pattern:** (WS) Working Row 1 of each patt, [work 3 sts in Slip-wrap, 7 (8, 9, 10) sts in L-Twist, 3 sts in Slip-wrap, 7 (8, 9, 10) sts in R-Twist] 4 times, end 3 sts in Slip-wrap. Work 7 rows even.

**Shape Bodice:** *Note: DO NOT inc each side of spines at side seam or center back markers—incs will be worked on a rep of Row 4 of the Twist patterns each time.*

(RS) Cont as est, inc 1 st (k-f/b) each side of princess line spines (see note above) this row, then every 8th row 2 times (3 times total), as foll: *Work as est to 1 st before spine, inc, work 3 sts as est, inc; rep from * for rem 3 princess line spines, working inc sts in patt as they become available—107 (115, 123, 131) sts. Cont as est until piece measures 9½″ from pick up row, end with a WS row.

### Divide for Underarm

(RS) Cont as est, work 26 (28, 30, 32) sts for right Front; join a new ball of yarn, leaving old ready for WS row, bind off 3 sts for underarm, work 49 (53, 57, 61) sts for Back; join new ball of yarn, bind off 3 sts for underarm, work 26 (28, 30, 32) sts for left Front.

## BACK

(WS) Working on Back sts only, cont in patt as est, work 1 row even.

**Shape Armholes:** (RS) At each armhole edge, dec 1 st EOR 5 (6, 6, 6) times as foll: If edge is in R-Twist, use k2tog; in L-Twist, use ssk—39 (41, 45, 49) sts for Back.

Work even until armhole measures 7 (7½, 8, 8½)" from Dividing Row—sleeve spine will be grafted to shoulder and adds additional ½" per side to each armhole.

**Shape Shoulders and Neck:** Bind off 4 (4, 4, 5) sts at beg of next 2 rows, 4 sts at beg next 2 rows, then 2 (3, 4, 4) sts at beg of next 2 rows for shoulders—19 (19, 21, 23) sts for neck. Bind off all sts.

## LEFT FRONT

(WS) Working on left Front sts only, work as for Back until armhole measures 6 (6½, 7, 7½)" from Dividing Row—21 (22, 24, 26) sts.

**Shape Front Neck:** Work Short Row Shaping as foll:

(RS) Work to 4 sts from end (1 st before Slip-wrap), wrap next st and turn (wrp-t). *(WS) Work even in patt as est, turn.

(RS) Work to 1 st before wrap, wrp-t. Rep from * 3 times more, and AT SAME TIME, when left Front measures same length as Back to shoulder, shape shoulders as for Back. Place 11 (11, 12, 13) neck sts from Short Row Shaping on holder.

## RIGHT FRONT

Work as for left Front reversing all shaping.

## CUFF

(make 2)

Worked side-to-side.

Using long-tail cast-on method, cast on 11 sts.

**Establish Pattern:** (WS) Working Row 1 of each patt, work 3 sts in Slip-wrap, 8 sts in L-Twist.

Cont in patt as est until piece is 4 (4, 4½, 4½)" long, end with (RS) Row 2 of Twist patt; pm for Sleeve seam.

**Shape Cuff:** Rep Short Row Shaping as per Hem, working from * to *.

**Establish Pattern:** (RS) Work R-Twist over 8 sts, work to end as est. Cont in patt as est, work even until shorter edge of piece measures 8 (8, 9, 9)" from beg, end with a WS row.

**Left Edging:** (RS) Bind off 7 sts, work to end as est—4 sts.

**Establish Pattern:** (WS) Work 3 sts as est, k1 (selvedge st).

Cont as est, work even until Slip-wrap "spine" measures same as bound off edge; bind off selvedge st, leave rem 3 sts on holder. Invisibly sew "spine" to bound off edge.

**Right Edging:** With RS facing, beg at cast on edge at opposite end of cuff, pick up and knit 3 sts in Slip-wrap sts, plus 1 st (selvedge st)—4 sts. Work as for Left Edging, working first (WS) row: K1, work 3 sts in Slip-wrap.

## SLEEVES

With RS facing, beg at marker for sleeve seam, working along shorter edge, pick up and knit 12 (12, 14, 14) sts to stitch holder, fold the cuff so that 2 stitch holders are placed one behind the other; knit the 3 sts on holders tog as foll: * Insert RH needle into st of top holder; rep from * twice —6 sts reduced to 3. (These 3 sts will become the Slip-wrap at center of Sleeve); pick up and knit 12 (12, 14, 14) sts to marker, turn—27 (27, 31, 31) sts.

**Establish Pattern:** (WS) Working Row 1 of each patt, work 12 (12, 14, 14) sts in L-Twist, 3 sts in Slip-wrap, 12 (12, 14, 14) sts in R-Twist. Cont in patt as est, work even for 5 rows, end with a WS row.

**Shape Sleeve:** Inc 1 st each side this row, then every 6th row for a total of 7 (8, 7, 8) times, working new sts in patt as they become est—41 (43, 45, 47) sts. Work even until piece measures 13" from pick up row, end with a WS row.

**Shape Sleeve Cap:** Bind off 2 sts beg next 2 rows—37 (39, 41, 43) sts. Dec 1 st at each armhole edge EOR 8 times, every row 6 times—9 (11, 13, 15) sts. Bind off 3 (4, 5, 6) sts at beg of next 2 rows—3 sts of spine rem at top of sleeve. Work even until spine measures 3¼ (3½, 4, 4¼)" from last shaping row; bind off.

## FINISHING

Set in Sleeves, sewing spine at top of Sleeve to shoulder shaping, Front and Back, to join shoulders. Sew sleeve seam.

## COLLAR

With RS facing, beg with 11 (11, 12, 13) sts on right Front neck holder, work 3 sts in Slip-wrap, k1, inc 1 (k-f/b) in each of the rem 7 (7, 8, 9) sts from holder; pick up and work 3 sts of right shoulder spine in Slip-wrap; pick up and knit 28 (28, 30, 32) sts evenly spaced across 19 (19, 21, 23) sts of Back neck; pick up and work 3 sts of left shoulder spine in Slip-wrap, inc 1 in each of next 6 (7, 8, 9) sts on left Front neck holder, k1, work rem 3 sts in Slip-wrap—70 (70, 74, 78) sts.

**Next Row:** (WS) Work 3 sts in Slip-wrap at Front edges and shoulders as est, work R-Twist over left side of neck to center Back, pm, work L-Twist over right side neck to last 3 sts, work 3 sts in Slip-wrap. Cont in patt as est until Collar measures 8" from pick up row. Fold Collar to inside and whipstitch in place; sew tog the folded spine at Collar edges.

Baste zipper along center Front, leaving the bottom hem open, aligning lower end of zipper with pick up row; zipper top is approx 1½" below Collar. Sew zipper to Front edges.

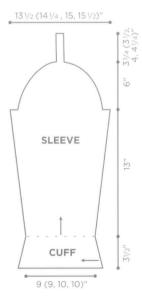

13½ (14¼, 15, 15½)"

3¼ (3½, 4, 4¼)"

6"

SLEEVE

13"

3½"

CUFF

9 (9, 10, 10)"

## LEFT DIAGONAL TWIST RIB
(even number of sts)

Repeat

## RIGHT DIAGONAL TWIST RIB
(even number of sts)

Repeat

## LEFT DIAGONAL TWIST RIB
(odd number of sts)

Repeat

## RIGHT DIAGONAL TWIST RIB
(odd number of sts)

Repeat

## KEY

 Knit on RS, purl on WS.

Purl on RS, knit on WS.

**Right Twist:** Wyib, knit into 2nd st (st on left, which will appear as knit st), but do not drop any sts off needle, wyif, purl into first st, slip pair off left needle tip.

**Left Twist:** Wyib open out left-hand needle so that WS (back loops) of sts are accessible, knit into back loop of 2nd st, but do not drop any sts off needle, wyib, knit into front loop of first st, slip pair off needle tip.

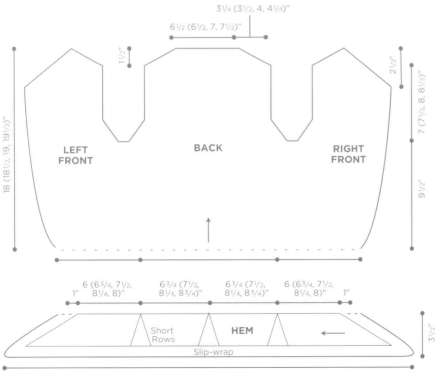

3¹⁄₄ (3¹⁄₂, 4, 4¹⁄₄)"

6¹⁄₂ (6¹⁄₂, 7, 7¹⁄₂)"

1¹⁄₂"

2¹⁄₂"

7 (7¹⁄₂, 8, 8¹⁄₂)"

18 (18¹⁄₂, 19, 19¹⁄₂)"

LEFT FRONT

BACK

RIGHT FRONT

9¹⁄₂"

6 (6³⁄₄, 7¹⁄₂, 8¹⁄₄, 8)" 1"

6³⁄₄ (7¹⁄₂, 8¹⁄₄, 8³⁄₄)"

6³⁄₄ (7¹⁄₂, 8¹⁄₄, 8³⁄₄)"

6 (6³⁄₄, 7¹⁄₂, 8¹⁄₄, 8)" 1"

Short Rows

HEM

Slip-wrap

3¹⁄₂"

36 (39, 41¹⁄₂, 44)"

# ragamuffin pullover and earflap hat

## pullover

### STITCH PATTERN

**Woven Motif** (see diagram at right) Make 3 slits over 8 rows, each slanted 1 st to left when seen from RS fabric, beg on row designated in patt below:

**Row 1:** (RS) Bind off 7 sts.

**Row 2:** Purl to where sts were bound off, cast on 7 sts using single cast on, purl to end.

**Row 3:** Knit.

**Row 4:** Purl until 1 st before where first st was cast on below, bind off 7 sts, purl to end.

**Row 5:** Knit to where the sts were bound off, cast on 7 sts, knit to end.

**Row 6:** Purl.

**Row 7:** Knit to where sts were cast on, then k1, bind off 7 sts, knit to end.

**Row 8:** Purl to where sts were bound off, cast on 7 sts, purl to end.

### BACK

Using long-tail cast-on method and 2 strands MC held together, cast on 50 (54, 58) sts.

---

**SIZES**
Small 2T–3T (Medium 4-5, Large 6-7)
Pullover and Hat shown in size Small.

**KNITTED MEASUREMENTS**
**pullover**
Hem: 28½ (31, 33)"
Chest: 24 (26, 28½)"
Length: 15 (16, 17)"
Sleeve at upper arm: 11 (12, 13)"

**hat**
19 (20¾)" around crown

**YARN**
**pullover**
Rowan "Rowanspun DK" (100% wool), DK tweed; use double strand
4 (5, 6) hanks (1.75oz/50g; 219yd/200m) in 750 thor (gray-brown) (MC)
1 hank each of 4 contrast colors (CCs) in 731 punch (orange) (A), 732 chili (red) (B)

Small amount in 747 catkin (green) (C)
Small amount Rowan "Felted Tweed" (50% merino/25% alpaca/25% viscose) 1.75oz/50g; 191yd/175m) in 139 crush (plum) (D)

**hat**
1 hank MC and small amount each of 4 CCs (see pullover)

**NEEDLES/TOOLS**
Tapestry needle (for pullover and hat)

**pullover**
US 10 (6mm) needles, or size to match gauge
US 6 (4mm) needles for trim
Stitch holders/spare circular needles

**hat**
US 6 (4mm) 16" long circular; 1 set US 6 (4mm) double-pointed needles (dpn), or size to match gauge
Cable needle

**GAUGE**
**pullover**
14 sts and 20 rows = 4" in St st using larger needles and 2 strands held tog

**hat**
28 sts and 32 rnds = 4" in Colorwork Braided Cable
22 sts and 28 rows = 4" in St st
Always check and MATCH gauge for best fit.

## FAIR ISLE TRIM

** (WS) Beg Garter st (knit every row); work even for 3 rows. Change to smaller needles.

Row 1: (RS) Break off 1 strand MC; using smaller needles and single strands of each color, with MC, knit into each strand of first st of previous row—2 sts worked in one st, using single strand A, knit into each strand of next st; cont in this manner, working 2 sts in each st, alternating MC and A to end of row, wrapping new color over previous color to prevent holes—100 (108, 116) sts.

Row 2: * Purl 2 A, purl 2 MC; rep from * to end.

Row 3: * K2 MC, k2 A; rep from * across. Break off A.

Row 4: Using MC, purl all sts. Change to larger needles and double strand MC.

Row 5: * P2tog; rep from * across, decreasing to original number of sts—50 (54, 58) sts.

Purl 3 rows—Garter st. **

### Shape Sides and place Motifs:

Row 1: (RS) Change to St st; dec 1 st each side every 6th row 4 times—42 (46, 50) sts will rem after shaping, and AT SAME TIME, place Motifs.

Row 11: (Row 1 of Woven Motif) (RS) K31 (32, 33), bind off 7, knit to end. Cont in St st on rem sts, complete Motif.

Row 19: K5 (6, 7), bind off 7 sts, knit to end; cont in St st on rem sts, complete Motif.

Work even until piece measures 8½ (9, 9½)" from beg, end with a WS row.

Shape Armholes: (RS) K1, k2tog, knit to last 3 sts, ssk, k1; work 1 row even.

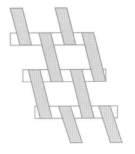

**WOVEN MOTIF**
(after weaving)

Next Row: (RS) (Row 1 of Motif)—K1, k2tog, k7, bind off 7 sts, knit to 3 sts before end, k2tog, k1; work 1 row even.

Cont as est, dec 1 st each side EOR 1 (2, 2) more times, while completing Motif—36 (38, 42) sts.

Work even until armhole measures 5½ (6, 6½)" from beg of shaping, end with a WS row.

Shape Shoulders: Bind off 3 sts at beg of next 2 (2, 4) rows, then 2 sts at beg of next 4 (4, 2) rows—22 (24, 26) for neck. Bind off rem sts.

### FRONT

Work as for Back until armhole measures 4 (4½, 5)", end with a WS row; pm each side of center 16 (18, 20) sts.

Shape Neck: (RS) Work across to marker, bind off center 16 (18, 20) sts; join a new double-strand ball and work to end. Work 1 row even. (RS) Working both sides at same time, at each neck edge, dec 1 st EOR 3 times, working decs 1 st in from edge (on left neck edge, work as ssk; on right neck edge, work as k2tog).

### COLLAR

Graft left shoulder seam. With RS facing, using larger needles and 2 strands MC, beg at right shoulder,

pick up and knit 22 (24, 26) sts across Back neck, 28 (30, 32) sts around Front neck edge—50 (54, 58) sts.

Fair Isle Trim: (WS) Work as for Back from ** to **, using B as the CC instead of A.

Bind off purlwise on last row of Garter st. Sew collar seam and graft right shoulder together.

### RIGHT SLEEVE

*Note: Sleeves are picked up and knit down so you can adjust length to fit child.*

With RS facing, using larger needle and 2 strands MC held together, beg above the armhole shaping at back, pick up and knit 32 (34, 38) sts along the straight edge of armhole, end at Front shaping. Beg St st; work 1 row even.

Shape Cap: (RS) Inc 1 st each side EOR 3 (4, 4) times—38 (42, 46) sts.

Shape Sleeve and place Motif: (RS) Dec 1 st each side every 6th row 6 (7, 8) times—26 (28, 30) sts. AT SAME TIME, when sleeve measures 4½" from pick up row, place Motif, 8 sts from beg of RS row.

Work even until sleeve measures 10¼ (12¼, 14¼)" or desired length minus 1¾", end with a RS row.

Fair Isle Trim: Work as for Back from ** to **. Bind off purlwise on last row of Garter st.

### LEFT SLEEVE

Work as for right Sleeve, picking up sts from Front to Back; place Motif 3" down from pick up row, centered on Sleeve.

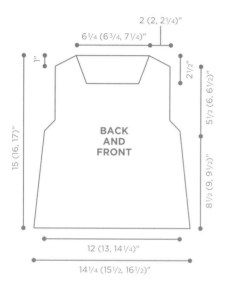

**Rnds 7 and 8:** Rep Rnds 3 and 4.

**Rnd 9:** Working colors as est, * C6F; rep from * around; break CCs.

Rep Rnds 2–9 for Colorwork Braided Cable.

### CROWN

Using circular needle, long-tail cast-on and MC, cast on 132 (144) sts. Pm on RH needle for beg of round. Join, being careful not to twist sts.

Beg St st (knit every rnd); work even for 3 rnds.

Beg Colorwork Braided Cable. Work even until piece measures 6 (7)" from beg, end Rnd 4 of patt.

**Shape Crown:** Decrease Rnd—* Slip 3 sts to cn, hold to front parallel with LH needle, insert RH needle knitwise into first st on cn and then into first st on LH needle, k2tog; [insert RH needle into next st on cn and then into next st on LH needle, k2tog] twice—3 sts decreased—cont as est, rep from * around—66 (72) sts. Changing to dpn when sts become too tight for circular needle, work 1 rnd even.

Rep the Decrease Rnd—33 (36) sts.

**Fringes:** Work 11 (12) fringes at center top of hat as follows: K3, turn. Cont on these 3 sts only, in St st (knit on RS, purl on WS), work even for 7 more rows; bind off. Join yarn of desired color to work next 3 sts; knit 8 rows in St st; bind off. Cont as est around. With WS facing, using tapestry needle and a double strand of yarn for strength, run yarn through last dec rnd to close hole below fringes.

### FINISHING
Block lightly with steam.

**Motifs:** Make 32 strips, 8 strips in each of the 4 CC as follows:

Cast on 2 sts, work in St st for 3", bind off. *Hint: Leave 3" tail at cast on and bind off ends for sewing.* Weave one strip of each color through the slits of each motif as shown in diagram—the strips alternately extend ½" above or below the top or bottom slit. Tack down using yarn tails.

### earflap hat
**SPECIAL TERMS**

**C6B:** Slip 3 sts to cn and hold to back, k3, k3 from cn.

**C6F:** Slip 3 sts to cn and hold to front, k3, k3 from cn.

### COLORWORK BRAIDED CABLE
(multiple of 6 sts; 8-rnd rep)

**Rnd 1:** * C6F; rep from * around.

**Rnds 2 and 6:** Knit, adding a small reel of contrast color (CC) across 3 sts randomly (over 3 sts as divided by the cable) a few times—you will soon discover that by adding color to the first or 2nd set of 3 sts of the cable, the contrast color will appear to be woven to the right or to the left—vary the placement for a pleasing effect.

**Rnds 3 and 4:** Knit, stranding the MC behind the CC sts (you'll have to pull CC across WS for each CC section).

**Rnd 5:** Working colors as est, * C6B; rep from * around to last 3 sts; work C6B over last 3 sts and first 3 sts of rnd, slipping marker and replacing in the same place; break CCs.

## EARFLAPS
(make 2)

With RS facing, using MC, pick up and knit 33 (37) sts along lower edge. Work even in St st until piece measures 1½ (2½)" from pick up row, end with a WS row.

**Shape Earflap:** (RS) K2, ssk, knit to last 4 sts, k2tog, k2. Work 1 row even.

Cont as est, dec 1 st each side EOR 6 (8) times more—21 sts. Dec 1 st each side every row 6 times, working WS row decs as foll: P2, p2tog, purl to last 4 sts, p2tog-tbl, p2—9 sts rem.

**Next Row:** (RS) K2, ssk, k1, pass the loop from ssk over knit st on RH needle, k2tog, k2—6 sts. Work 1 row even.

## FRINGE
Knit 3, turn; cont in St st on these 3 sts only until fringe measures 4" or desired length. Bind off. Join yarn of desired color, work rem 3 sts as first 3 sts.

## LINING
With WS facing, using MC, pick up and knit 33 (37) sts along pick up edge of the earflap. (WS) Beg St st; Cont in St st, adding a few stripes of CC as desired; when Lining measures same as Earflap to beg of shaping, end with a WS row.

Shape Lining as for Earflap; work 2 fringes as for Earflap.

Using tapestry needle and 1 strand MC, sew Earflap to Lining along all sides.

Make another Earflap spaced as follows: Leave 21 (24) sts at Back of hat and 45 (48) sts at Front and pick up 33 (37) sts at opposite side of hat.

# unisex basketweave v-neck and scarf

## SIZES
Men's/Unisex Small (Medium, Large)

To fit Chest 38–42 (44–46, 48–52)

V-neck shown in Small.

## KNITTED MEASUREMENTS

**v-neck**
Chest: 45 (49 ½, 56)"

Length: 26 ½ (27, 27 ½)"

Sleeve at upper arm: 19 ½ (20 ½, 21 ¼)"

**scarf**
8 ½" wide x 60" long

## YARN
Goddess "Jay" (70% wool/ 30% alpaca), 2-ply bulky

**v-neck**
9 (11, 13) skeins (3.5oz/100g; 87yd/80m) in 0713 field (straw yellow)

**scarf**
2 skeins in 7255 summer squash (MC)

1 skein each in 6396 peacock (A), 3983 pansy (B), 5141 violet (C), and 2266 merlot (D)

## NEEDLES/TOOLS
US 11 (8mm) 24" long circular, or size to match gauge

Crochet hook J-10 (6mm)

## GAUGE
10 sts and 16 rows = 4" over large-scale basketweave pattern

Always check and MATCH gauge for best fit.

## OVERVIEW
This sweater is worked straight on circular needles; the sleeves are knit down from shoulder to allow for custom fit. The V-neck is engineered to divide a column of knits in the stitch pattern.

For the scarf, use separate balls for each color block, as per Intarsia. The MC is always knit on RS, purl on WS; the contrast colors are purl on RS, knit on WS. When working the first row of CC over a block of MC, knit all sts on RS.

*Note: Leave long tails of each color at beg and end of each color block. After Scarf is completed, pull the tail through one loop on WS, then leave hanging out and trim to approx 2". The side with all the tails is called WS in the instructions, but either side can face out when worn.*

## v-neck
### SPECIAL TECHNIQUE
**Decrease in Pattern (dec):** At armhole edges: Work 2 sts as est, dec in patt over next 2 sts as foll: Work dec on 3rd and 4th st, using dec that slants toward armhole—if the 2nd st of next pair of sts is a knit, work dec as k2tog, if a purl, work ssp; work in patt as est to last 4 sts—if the first st of next pair of sts is a knit, work dec as ssk, if a purl, work p2tog; work rem 2 sts in patt.

### BACK
Using long-tail cast-on method, cast on 56 (62, 70) sts. (RS) Beg Large-Scale Basketweave from Chart, Row 1.

**Establish Pattern:** P0 (0, 4), k3 (6, 6), work 14-st rep 3 (4, 4) times, end p8 (0, 4), k3 (0, 0).

Work even until piece measures 15 ½" from beg, end with a WS row.

**Shape Armhole:** (RS) Beg this row, dec 1 st each side EOR 4 (5, 5) times, working decs in patt—48 (52, 60) sts. Cont as est, work even until armhole measures 9 ½ (10, 10 ½)" from beg of shaping, end with a WS row.

**Shape Shoulders:** Bind off 5 (5, 6) sts at beg of next 4 rows, 4 (5, 6) sts at beg next 2 rows for shoulders—20 (22, 24) sts rem for neck; bind off all sts.

## FRONT

Work as for Back until piece measures 21" from beg (armhole measures 5½" from beg of shaping), end with (WS) Row 4 of Chart. (*Note: In order to have the neck shaping beg in the center of a St st block, it is necessary to have a 6-st knit block at center Front, with 1" of the block completed; the block will be divided at the center and 3 knit sts will cont up the edges of the V-neck, with dec worked in patt inside the edge sts—48 [52, 60] sts.*)

**Divide for V-neck:** (RS) Work 20 (22, 26) sts as est (1 purl st rem before center St st block), k2tog (the first st of St st block with the purl st), k2; join a new ball of yarn, k2, ssk (the last st of St st block with the next purl st), work to end as est.

Working both sides at same time with separate balls of yarn, work 1 row even.

**Shape neck:** (RS) On left Front, work across to last 4 sts, k2tog, k2; on right Front, k2, ssk, work to end. Work 1 row even, working 3 neck edge sts in St st. Cont as est, at each neck edge, dec 1 st each side EOR 8 (9, 10) times more for a total of 10 (11, 12) decs each side; AT SAME TIME, when armhole measures 9½ (10, 10½)" from beg of shaping, end with a WS row.

Shape shoulders as for Back.

Graft shoulder seams.

### RIGHT SLEEVE

With RS facing, beg at right Back armhole above shaping, pick up and knit 41 (41, 43) sts along straight edge, end at shaping on Front armhole. (WS) Beg Row 2, work Small-Scale Basketweave from Chart, beg and end where indicated for your size; AT SAME TIME,

**Shape Cap:** (RS) Inc 1 st each side EOR 4 (5, 5) times (to match underarm decs), working new sts into patt as they become established—49 (51, 53) sts.

**Shape Sleeves:** Dec 1 st each side every 6th row 10 (10, 6) times, every 4th row 0 (0, 6) times—29 (31, 31) sts. Work even until sleeve measures 21 (19, 18)" from pick up, bind off rem sts.

## LEFT SLEEVE

Work as for right Sleeve, beg at left Front armhole, working along straight edge to Back.

## FINISHING

Block lightly. Sew side seams, leaving 4" open at bottom hem for side slits. Sew Sleeve seams and sew Sleeve cap edges to armhole shaping.

**Edging:** Using crochet hook, work 1 row single crochet along Back neck and side vents.

## scarf

Using long-tail cast-on method and separate balls of yarn, leaving 4" tails for each color, cast on 3 sts MC, 8 sts A, 6 sts MC, 4 sts B—21 sts.

**Row 1:** (WS) K4 with B, p6 with MC, k8 with A, p3 with MC; bring each new color around the previous color, as per Intarsia, in order to prevent holes.

**Row 2:** K3 with MC, p8 with A, k6 with MC, p4 with B.

Rep Rows 1 and 2 twice, then work Row 1 once more—a total of 7 rows, plus the cast on row, which counts as the 8th row for these blocks. Leaving

4" tails, cut CC A and B. Join C and D, leaving 4" tails.

**\*\* Row 8:** K4 with C, k6 with MC, k8 with D, k3 with MC.

Cont as est, working MC in St st, CC in Rev St st for a total of 8 rows.

**Row 16:** K3 with MC, k8 with B, k6 with MC, k4 with A.

Cont as est, working MC in St st, CC in Rev St st for a total of 8 rows.

**Row 24:** K4 with D, k6 with MC, k8 with C, k3 with MC.

Cont as est, working MC in St st, CC in Rev St st for a total of 8 rows.

**Row 32:** K3 with MC, k8 with A, k6 with MC, k4 with B.

Cont as est, working MC in St st, CC in Rev St st for a total of 8 rows.

Rep from **\*\*** for Color Block patt.

Work even in Color Block patt until scarf measures 60" from the beg, end with a RS row, with 1 row left to complete a set of Color Blocks.

(WS) Bind off purlwise, using colors as est in each area. Secure ends on WS (see Overview).

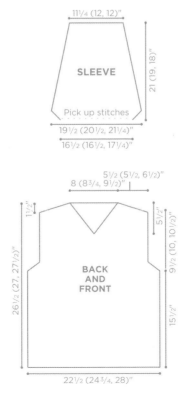

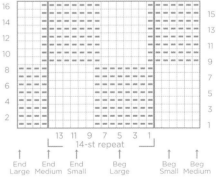

**LARGE-SCALE BASKETWEAVE**

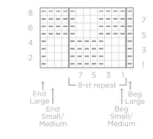

**SMALL-SCALE BASKETWEAVE**

**KEY**

☐ Knit on RS, purl on WS. ⊟ Purl on RS, knit on WS.

# braided-bodice wench blouse

**CABLES**
(See Charts)

**BACK**
Using long-tail cast-on method, cast on 80 (88, 96) sts.

**Hem:** (WS) Beg St st (knit on RS, purl on WS); work even for 7 rows.

(RS) Beg Chart A; work Rows 1–3 once. (WS) Beg St st; work even until piece measures 12½ (13, 13)" from beg, end with a WS row.

**Shape Armholes:** (RS) Bind off 3 sts at beg of next 2 rows—74 (82, 90) sts.

Dec 1 st each side every other row 6 times—62 (70, 78) sts.

Work even until armhole measures 7½ (8, 8½)" from beg of shaping, end with a WS row.

**Shape Shoulders and Neck:** (RS) Bind off 8 sts beg of next 0 (2, 4) rows, 6 sts beg of next 6 (4, 2) rows—26 (30, 34) sts rem for neck; bind off rem sts.

**FRONT**
Work as for Back until piece measures 4½ (5, 5½)" from beg, end with a RS row.

**Establish Pattern:** (WS) Work in St st as est across 30 (34, 38) sts, pm, [p-f/b, k1] 10 times, pm, work in St st to end—90 (98, 106) sts.

(RS) Beg Chart B, Row 1, on center 30 sts, working sts each side of Chart in St st throughout. Work even as est through Row 32 of Chart B. Beg Chart C on center 30 sts; work Rows 33–36.

**Row 37:** Work to center chart, join a new ball of yarn and work to end.

**SIZES**
Small (Medium, Large)
**Shown in Small.**

**KNITTED MEASUREMENTS**
**Chest:** 35½ (39, 42)"
**Waist:** 26½ (30, 33)"
**Length:** 21 (22, 22½)"
**Sleeve at upper arm:** 12 (13, 14)" (where smocked)

**YARN**
Crystal Palace "Cotton Chenille" (100% cotton), worsted weight chenille 9 (9, 10) hanks (1.75oz/ 50g; 98yd/89m) in 9253 lavender

*Note: You may wish to use sport-weight wool yarn to sew seams as chenille is not very flexible and seams could break if stressed.*

**NEEDLES/TOOLS**
US 6 (4mm), or size to match gauge
Cable needle (cn)
Stitch markers
Tapestry needle
Crochet hook size H-8 (5mm)

**NOTIONS**
1½" button

**GAUGE**
18 sts and 24 rows = 4" in St st
24 sts = 4" over 4-st cables (hems)
30 sts = 4" over 6-st cables (bodice)
Always check and MATCH gauge for best results.

Working both sides at same time with separate balls of yarn, work 1 row even.

**Row 39:** Beg neck shaping from Chart, working Cables and dec each side of neck edge as shown. Dec 1 st EOR a total of 12 (12, 14) times (8 are shown on chart); and AT SAME TIME, when piece measures same as Back to underarm, shape armhole as for Back (approx 2 [2, 1½]" above beg neck shaping)—24 (26, 28) sts rem for each shoulder after neck and armhole shaping is completed. And AT SAME TIME, when neck measures 5½ (6, 6)" from beg of shaping, end with a WS row. Discontinue the 6-st Cables at neck edges.

### CABLED SMOCKING

On left Front sts:

**Row 1:** (RS) Work K0 (2, 0), C4F 6 (6, 7) times.

**Row 2:** Purl.

**Row 3:** K2 (4, 2), C4B 5 (5, 6) times, k2.

On right Front sts:

**Row 1:** (RS) Work C4B 6 (6, 7) times, k0 (2, 0).

**Row 2:** Purl.

**Row 3:** K2, C4F 5 (5, 6) times, end k2 (4, 2).

**Work 5 rows St st, then rep Rows 1–3 of Cabled Smocking; rep from ** once more (19 rows); and AT SAME

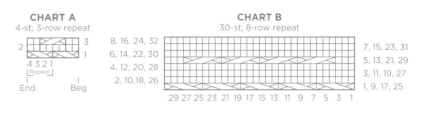

**CHART A**
4-st; 3-row repeat

**CHART B**
30-st; 8-row repeat

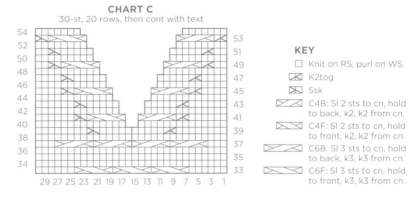

**CHART C**
30-st; 20 rows, then cont with text

**KEY**
☐ Knit on RS, purl on WS.
⤬ K2tog
⤬ Ssk
C4B: Sl 2 sts to cn, hold to back, k2, k2 from cn.
C4F: Sl 2 sts to cn, hold to front, k2, k2 from cn.
C6B: Sl 3 sts to cn, hold to back, k3, k3 from cn.
C6F: Sl 3 sts to cn, hold to front, k3, k3 from cn.

TIME, when armhole measures same as Back to shoulder shaping, end with a WS row.

**Shape Shoulders:** At each shoulder, bind off 10 sts 0 (1, 2) times, 8 sts 3 (2, 1) times. *Note: Different shoulder shaping than Back is because Cable Smocking pulls in.*

### SLEEVES

Cast on 56 (60, 64) sts and work Hem as for Back; beg St st.

Work even until piece measures 2½" from Hem, end with a RS row.

**Next Row:** (WS) Inc 16 (18, 20) sts evenly across row—72 (78, 84) sts. Work 1" in St st, end with a WS row.

**Establish Pattern:** (RS) Work C6F 12 (13, 14) times across.

Work 3 rows even in St st.

**Next Row:** (RS) K3, C6B 11 (12, 13) times, k3; work 1 (WS) row, dec 0 (2, 4) sts evenly across—72 (76, 80) sts.

Work even until piece measures 15½" from beg, end with a WS row.

(RS) Beg Chart A; work Rows 1–3 once. (WS) Purl 1 row dec 12 (14, 14) sts evenly across—60 (64, 68) sts.

Work even until piece measures 20" from beg, end with a WS row.

**Shape Sleeve Cap:** Bind off 3 sts beg next 2 rows—54 (58, 62) sts. Dec 1 st each side EOR 14 times, every row 6 times—14 (18, 22) sts; bind off rem sts.

### FINISHING

Sew shoulder seams, easing sts together. Sew sleeve and side seams, leaving left side seam open at lower edge for 2½". Set in sleeves. With RS facing, using crochet hook, single crochet into each st of Back Neck. Weave in ends. Sew button to Back at left side seam above Hem where Chart A worked; using a double strand of yarn, make a loop and sew opposite button.

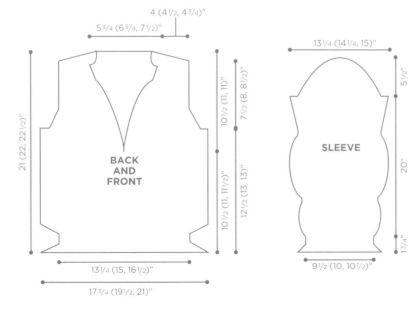

BACK AND FRONT

SLEEVE

# yarn-over steek vest

## SIZES

Small (Medium, Large)
*Note that fabric is very stretchy when choosing size.*
**Shown in Small.**

## KNITTED MEASUREMENTS

**Chest:** 30 (33¼, 36¾)"
**Waist:** 27¼ (30½, 33¾)"
**Length:** 21 (22¼, 22¾)"

## YARN

GGH/Meunch "Bergamo" (100% wool), bulky tubular ribbon
4 (5, 6) balls (1.75oz/50g; 66yd/60m) in 3910 magenta

## NEEDLES/TOOLS

US 15 (10mm) 24" long circular, or size to match gauge
Stitch holder/spare circular needle
Tapestry needle

## GAUGE

10 sts and 12 rows = 4" in St st
Always check and MATCH gauge for best fit.

## SPECIAL TECHNIQUE

**Yarn-Over Steek:** Bring yarn to front between needles, wrap yarn over the RH needle—be sure wrap encompasses fullest part of needle, not merely the tip—from front to back (continue to wrap as many times as indicated), keep yarn to back if next st is knit, bring to front if a purl and continue to work to end of round/row. On next round/row drop previous wrap and work Yarn-Over Steek at same place.

## BODY

Using long-tail cast-on method, cast on 68 (76, 84) sts. Pm on RH needle for beg of round. Join, being careful not to twist sts. Beg 2x2 Rib; work until piece measures 3" from beg, dec 4 sts on last rnd to align rib for Steek as foll:

K2tog, (p2, k2) 7 (8, 9) times, p2, k2tog, pm for side, p2tog, (k2, p2) 7 (8, 9) times, k2, p2tog—64 (72, 80) sts. Change to St st (knit every rnd).

**Rnds 1–12:** K16 (18, 20), yo 1 time, knit to end.

**Rnd 13:** K14 (16, 18), k2tog, yo 2 times, ssk, knit to end.

**Rnds 14–26:** K15 (17, 19), yo 2 times, knit to end.

**Rnd 27:** K13 (15, 17), k2tog, yo 3 times, ssk, knit to end.

**Rnds 28–32:** K14 (16, 18), yo 3 times, knit to end—piece measures 14" from beg.

**Divide Front/Shape Armholes:** Bind off 2 sts (this takes 3 sts, 1 rem on RH needle), k11 (13, 15), yo 3 times, k14 (16, 18) for Front. Beg working in rows, placing 32 (36, 40) sts of Back on spare needle or stitch holder.

**Row 34:** (WS) Working on Front sts only, bind off 2 sts (this takes 3 sts, 1 is left on needle), p11 (13, 15), yo 3 times, p12 (14, 16)—24 (28, 32) sts.

**Row 35:** (RS) K1, ssk, k9 (11, 13), yo 3 times, knit to last 3 sts, k2tog, k1.

**Row 36:** P11 (13, 15), yo 3 times, purl to end.

**Row 37:** K1, ssk, k8 (10, 12), yo 3 times, knit to last 3 sts, k2tog, k1.

**Row 38:** P10 (12, 14), yo 3 times, purl to end.

**Row 39:** K1, ssk, k7 (9, 11), yo 4 times, knit to last 3 sts, k2tog, k1.

**Row 40:** P9 (11, 13), yo 4 times, purl to end.

**Row 41:** K9 (11, 13), yo 4 times, knit to end.

Cont as est, rep Rows 40 and 41, 2 (3, 4) times, then row 40 once more.

**Shape Left Neck and Shoulder:** (RS) K9 (11, 13) for left neck; leave rem sts on holder for right neck.

**Row 1 and all WS rows:** Purl.

**Rows 2 and 4:** Knit to last 3 sts, k2tog, k1—7 (9, 11) sts.

**Row 6:** Bind off 3 (4, 4) sts for shoulder, knit to last 3 sts k2tog, k1—3 (4, 6) sts.

**Row 8:** Bind off 3 (3, 4) sts for shoulder—0 (1, 2) sts; size Small: Cut yarn.

**Sizes Medium and Large:** Rep Row 1, then bind off rem 1 (2) sts.

**Shape Right Neck and Shoulder:** With RS facing, join yarn at right neck edge; work as for left neck, reversing neck and shoulder shaping, by making neck decreases on first 3 sts of RS rows (k1, ssk) and binding off for shoulder at beg of WS rows.

**BACK**
With RS facing, join yarn at underarm. Beg St st (knit on RS, purl on WS).

**Shape Armhole:** Bind off 2 sts at beg of next 2 rows—28 (32, 36) sts.

Dec 1 st each side EOR 3 times as for Front—22 (26, 30) sts.

Work even until armhole measures the same as Front to shoulders, end with a WS row.

Shape right Shoulder as foll:

**Next row:** (RS) Bind off 3 (4, 4) sts for shoulder (this takes 4 [5, 5] sts, 1 remains on needle), k2 (3, 5), turn.

(WS) Purl these 3 (4, 6) sts.

(RS) Bind off 3 (3, 4) sts for shoulder—0 (1, 2) sts; size Small: Cut yarn.

**Sizes Medium and Large:** Purl 1 row, then bind off rem 1 (2) sts.

Place center 10 (12, 10) sts on holder for neck.

**Shape Left Shoulder:** With WS facing, join yarn at left shoulder and work as for right shoulder.

**FINISHING**
Sew shoulder seams.

# cashmere lace blouse

**SIZE**
Small (Medium, Large)
**Shown in Small.**

**KNITTED
MEASUREMENTS**
Chest: 36 (39, 42)"
Waist: 25 (27½, 30)"—rib
unstretched
Length: 20½ (21, 21½)"
Sleeve at upper arm: 12
(13¾, 15¼)"

**YARN**
Joseph Galler "Pashmina
Group II" (100% superfine
cashmere), four cabled 2-ply
strands
7 (8, 9) hanks (1.75oz/50g;
170yd/155m) in 1146 citron

**NEEDLES/TOOLS**
US 2 (2.75mm) 24" long circular, or size to match gauge
(Garment is worked in rows
but circular needle facilitates
short rows)

Stitch holder or spare
circular needle
Tapestry needle

**GAUGE**
42 sts and 40 rows = 4" in
1x1 Rib, unstretched
30 sts and 42 rows = 4" in
English Lace
Always check and MATCH
gauge for best fit.

**OVERVIEW**

While the Back and Sleeve pieces of this sweater are straightforward, the Front features top-aligned short rows that curve the ribbed waistband so it is highest at center; bottom-aligned short rows are then worked at each side within the lace pattern to compensate. The ribbed front bands, which are picked up and knit into the center, also employ short rows to extend at the neck.

**BACK**

Cast on 133 (145, 157) sts. (WS) Beg 1x1 Rib as foll: * P1, k1; rep from * to last st, p1. Cont in Rib as est, work even until piece measures 3" from beg, end with a WS row.

(RS) Change to English Lace from Chart; beg and end as shown, work 22 (24, 26) 6-st reps across.

Work even as est until piece measures 12" from beg, end with a WS row.

**Shape Armholes:** (RS) Bind off 6 sts at beg of next 2 rows, then dec 1 st each side EOR 6 times—109 (121, 133) sts.

Work even until armhole measures 7½ (8, 8½)" from beg of shaping, end with a WS row.

**Shape Shoulders:** Work 3 Short Rows (see page 171) at each side, leaving 7 (8, 9) sts at armhole edge each time (21 [24, 27] sts each shoulder). Work in 1x1 Rib ¼" on all sts, working wraps tog with wrapped sts on first row. Bind off in Rib.

**FRONT**

**Waistband:** Cast on and work as for Back until piece measures 3" from beg, end with a WS row.

(RS) **Beg Short Row Shaping:** Cont as est, work to 6 sts from end of row, wrp-t. Work to 7 sts from end, wrp-t.

* Work to 5 sts from last wrap, wrp-t; rep from * until 10 (11, 12) wraps to each side, spaced 6 sts apart; 11 sts rem at center Front between final 2 wraps, end with a WS row, wrp-t.

(RS) Work across to end of row, working wraps tog with wrapped sts.

Leave the center 11 sts plus 61 (67, 73) sts for Left Front on spare needle or holder.

### RIGHT FRONT
Short Rows worked in English Lace will fill the space created by Short Row ribbing.

**Short Row 1:** P7, wrp-t. Work Row 1, Sts 1–6, then St 13 of Chart.

**Short Row 2:** P13, wrp-t. Work Row 3, Sts 1–13.

**Short Row 3:** P19, wrp-t. Work Row 5, Sts 1–7, then 2–13.

**Short Row 4:** P25, wrp-t. Work row 7, Sts 1–7, 2–7, then 2–13.

Cont working Short Rows, working patt from Chart, always incorporating 6 more sts (1 more rep), until 61 (67, 73) sts are being worked. Work even in patt from Chart until piece measures 12" from beg, end with a RS row.

**Shape Armhole:** (WS) At armhole edge (beg of WS row), bind off 6 sts once, then dec 1 st EOR 12 times (these extra decs are to accommodate extra width neckband)—43 (49, 55) sts.

Work even until armhole measures 7½ (8, 8½)" from beg of shaping, end with Row 4 or 8 of Chart.

**Shape Shoulder:** (RS) * K1, p2tog; rep from * to last st, k1—22 (25, 28) sts. Cont in 1x1 rib as est for ¼". Bind off.

### LEFT FRONT
Return sts from holder to needle, ready to work a WS row. Join yarn; bind off 11 center sts, purl across to end, working wraps tog with wrapped sts.

Beg Short Rows in English Lace pattern.

**Short Row 1:** Work Row 1, Sts 1–6, then St 13, wrp-t. P7.

**Short Row 2:** Work Row 3, Sts 1–13, wrp-t. P13.

**Short Row 3:** Work Row 5, Sts 1–7, then 2–13, wrp-t. P19.

**Short Row 4:** Work Row 7, Sts 1–7, 2–7, then 2–13, wrp-t. P25.

Cont working Short Rows, working patt from Chart, always incorporating 6 more sts (1 more rep), until 61 (67, 73) sts are being worked. Work as for right Front, reversing shaping.

### RIGHT FRONT BAND
With RS facing, beg at center Front waist, pick up and knit 103 (109, 115) sts along Front edge, ending 2½" before shoulder bind off (skip approx every 4th row). Beg 1x1 Rib and Short Rows as foll: (WS) [Rib 8 sts, wrp-t. Work as est to end] 9 (9, 10) times. Then cont in Rib on all sts until Band measures 2½" at neck edge, 1" at waist edge from pick up row, end with a WS row. (RS) Bind off loosely knitwise.

### LEFT FRONT BAND
With RS facing, beg 2½" down from shoulder, pick up and knit 103 (109, 115) sts, ending at center Front waist. Beg 1x1 rib; (WS) Work 1 row even. (RS) Beg Short Rows; work as for right Front Band.

## ENGLISH LACE CHART
6-st; 8-row repeat

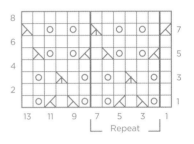

### KEY

☐ Knit on RS, purl on WS.

Ⓞ Yo

◩ K2tog

◪ Ssk

◪ Sk2p: Slip 1, k2tog, PSSO

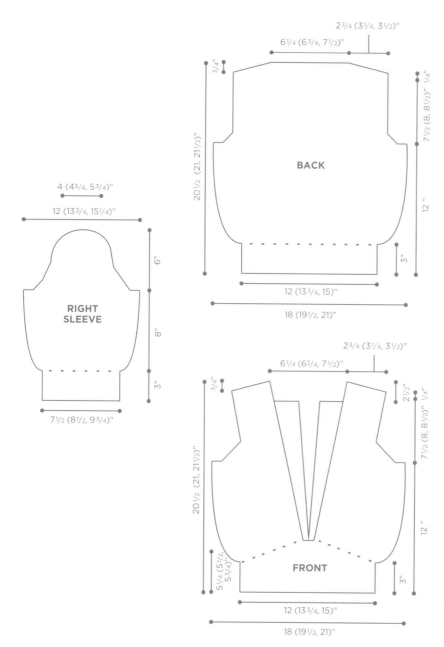

**RIGHT SLEEVE**

Using long-tail cast-on method, cast on 79 (91, 103) sts. (WS) Beg 1x1 Rib as foll: * P1, k1; rep from * to last st, p1. Cont in 1x1 Rib as est, work even until piece measures 3" from beg, end with a WS row.

(RS) Change to English Lace from Chart; beg and end as shown.

**Shape Sleeve:** (RS) Inc 1 st each side every 10th row 6 times—91 (103, 115) sts, working new sts in patt as they become est. Cont in Lace patt, work even until piece measures 11" from beg, end with a WS row.

**Shape Sleeve Cap:** (RS) Bind off 6 sts at beg of next 2 rows, then dec 1 st each side EOR 6 times—67 (79, 91) sts. At Front edge only (beg of RS rows), dec 1 st EOR 6 more times, and at Back edge, work: no dec, size Small (every 4th row 3 times, size Medium; EOR 6 times, size Large); then dec 1 st EOR 6 times at Back edge, and at Front edge, work: no dec, size Small (every 4th row 3 times, size Medium; EOR 6 times, size Large). Dec 1 st each side EOR 12 times more, bind off rem 31 (37, 43) sts.

**LEFT SLEEVE**

Work as for right Sleeve, reversing all shaping.

**FINISHING**

Sew Right Front Band over Left at waist fitting into 11 bound off sts at center front. Graft shoulder seam. Sew side and sleeve seams. Set in sleeves.

# lace leaf pullover

## SIZES
Small (Medium, Large)
**Shown in Small.**

## KNITTED MEASUREMENTS
**Chest:** 38 (42, 46)"
**Length:** 22 (22½, 23)"
**Sleeve at upper arm:** 13½ (14½, 15½)"

## YARN
Needful Yarns/Filtes King "Van Dyck" (46% wool/39% acrylic/15% alpaca), bulky of 6 single and two 2-ply strands

5 (6, 7) balls (3.5oz/100g; 117yd/107m) in 165 green heather

## NEEDLES/TOOLS
US 13 (9mm) 24" long and 32" long circular, or size to match gauge

Stitch markers

Stitch holders/spare circular needle
Tapestry needle

## NOTIONS
1 ceramic toggle button, ½" x 1" rectangle

## GAUGE
10 sts and 14 rows = 4" in St st

Always check and MATCH gauge for best fit.

## OVERVIEW
The sweater body is constructed in 2 pieces, the lower half is worked from the hem up, then the upper half is worked from the top down (partially in rows, partially in rnds), and then the pieces are grafted together—this allows for the leaf motif to extend from the ribbing of each piece; sleeves are knit from cuff up and grafted to the saddle shoulder. *Note: When working in rnds, read Chart from right to left for every rnd, every other rnd is knit even; when working Chart in rows (on upper body and left sleeve), read RS rows from right to left, WS rows from left to right, WS rows will be purled.*

## PATTERN STITCHES
### Twisted Rib
**Rnd/Row 1:** *K1-tbl, p1-tbl; rep from * across, ending k1-tbl if an odd number of sts.

**Rnd/Row 2:** Knit the knits-tbl, purl the purls-tbl as they face you.

Rep Rnd/Row 2 for Twisted Rib.

### Lace Pattern
(for Right Sleeve [panel of 7 sts])

**Row 1:** (RS) Yo, k2tog, k3, ssk, yo.

**Row 2:** Purl.

Rep Rows 1 and 2 for Lace patt.

## LOWER BODY
Using long-tail cast-on method and longer circular needle, cast on 96 (102, 108) sts. Pm on RH needle for beg of round (left side seam). Join, being careful not to twist sts. Beg Twisted Rib; work even for 7 rnds.

**Establish Pattern:** K25 (26, 27), pm, k15 for Leaf Chart, pm, k8 (10, 12), pm (right side seam), k48 (51, 54) sts for Back.

Cont as est, work Leaf Chart, beg Row 1, between markers on Front and rem sts in St st (knit every rnd). Work even as est until 17 rows of Leaf Chart are completed, then work all sts in St st until piece measures 9" from beg. Place sts on spare needle, keeping markers for side seams—or you can knit a few rows with scrap yarn and bind off—later the live sts will be grafted to bound off edge of Upper Body with Kitchener stitch.

## UPPER BODY

Using long-tail cast-on method and shorter circular needle, cast on 54 (58, 62) sts. (WS) Beg Twisted Rib; work even for 2 rows.

**Buttonhole Row:** (WS) K1-tbl, p1-tbl, yo, k2tog, work to end as est. Work 3 more rows in Twisted Rib, end with a RS row.

**Buttonhole Tab:** (WS) Bind off 4 sts, purl to end—50 (54, 58) sts.

**Next Row:** (RS) Increase Row—K5 (6, 7), pm for left Back shoulder; inc (k-f/b), k18 (19, 20) for Back neck, inc; pm for right Back shoulder, k5 (6, 7), pm for right Front shoulder; inc, k6 (7, 8), pm, work Row 1 of Chart (only 12 sts remain, but incs will accommodate remainder of Chart) to last st, inc in last st, pm; and instead of turning for WS row, fold needle and join to work in rnds—54 (58, 62) sts. Work 1 rnd even in St st, slipping markers (sl m).

**Next Rnd:** Increase Rnd—Sl m for beg of rnd, k5 (6, 7), sl m for left Back shoulder, inc, k20 (21, 22) for Back neck, inc, sl m for right Back shoulder, k5 (6, 7), sl m for right Front shoulder, inc, k7 (8, 9), sl m, work Row 3 of Chart, inc in last st. Work 1 rnd even.

Work in patt as est, cont to inc 1 st at each shoulder marker EOR a total of 5 (6, 7) times (the last Increase Rnd will be on Rnd 9 (11, 13) of Chart)—70 (78, 86) sts.

**Dividing Row:** (WS) On next row, which would be a knit-even rnd from RS, turn and purl across 30 (33, 36) sts, leaving yarn hanging, ready to work RS row; place next 5 (6, 7) sts on holder for shoulder (these will be grafted to top of sleeves); join new yarn and purl across 30 (33, 36) sts; place rem 5 (6, 7) sts on holder for shoulder.

Working each section separately, cont as est, completing Chart, and AT SAME TIME, inc 1 st each side every 4th row 5 times—40 (43, 46) sts. After completing these 20 rows of shaping and both sections are even in length, end with a WS row.

**Joining Rnd:** (RS) Work across first section, cast-on 8 sts for underarm (using single cast on); using same yarn, work across rem sts, cast on 8 sts for other underarm and join—96 (102, 108) sts.

Work even in St st for 4" more. Bind off.

## LEFT SLEEVE

Using long-tail cast-on method and shorter circular needle, cast on 23 (24, 25) sts. (WS) Beg Twisted Rib; work even for 8 rows. (WS) Purl 1 row.

**Establish Pattern:** (RS) K4 (4, 5), pm, work Row 1 of Chart over center 15 sts, pm, k4 (5, 5). Cont as est, working sts each side of Chart in St st, work 7 rows even.

**Shape Sleeve:** (RS) Inc 1 st each side this row, then every 8th row 5 (6, 7) times total—33 (36, 39) sts. Work even until piece measures 19" from beg, end with a WS row.

**Shape Sleeve Cap:** Bind off 4 sts beg of next 2 rows—25 (28, 31) sts.

Dec 1 st each side EOR 10 (9, 8) times, every row 0 (2, 4) times as foll: Work the decs on 2nd and 3rd sts in from edge using right slant (k2tog on RS; p2tog on WS) on RH side of piece, and left slant (ssk on RS; ssp on WS) on left side, end with a WS row—5 (6, 7) sts. Place sts on holder.

## RIGHT SLEEVE

Using long-tail cast-on method and shorter needle, cast on 23 (24, 25) sts. (WS) Beg Twisted Rib; work even for 8 rows. (WS) Purl 1 row. Work as for Left Sleeve, but instead of Leaf Chart on center 15 sts, work Lace patt on center 7 sts of Sleeve.

**Establish Pattern:** (RS) K8 (8, 9), pm, work Row 1 of Lace patt over center 7 sts, pm, k8 (9, 9).

## FINISHING

Using tapestry needle and Kitchener stitch, graft Lower Body and Upper Body pieces together; side seam of Lower Body should be centered under 8 underarm sts of Upper Body. Sew sleeve seam. Set in sleeves. Graft 5 (6, 7) sts on Sleeve holder to 5 (6, 7) sts on holder for shoulder.

Sew button to Collar rib at left shoulder.

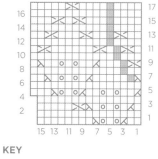

**LACE LEAF CHART**

**KEY**

☐ Knit on RS, purl on WS.

☒ K2tog

☒ Ssk

◉ Yo

▨ No stitch

⧗ **Right Twist:** Wyib, knit into 2nd st, but do not drop off needle, wyib knit into first st, slip pair off left needle tip.

⧗ **Left Twist:** Wyib, open out left-hand needle so that WS (back loops) of sts are accessible, knit into the back loop of 2nd st, but do not drop any sts off needle, wyib knit into front loop of first st, slip pair off needle tip.

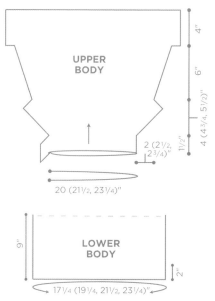

UPPER BODY

4"

6"

4 (4¾, 5½)"

1½"

2 (2½, 2¾)"

20 (21½, 23¼)"

LOWER BODY

9"

2"

17¼ (19¼, 21½, 23¼)"

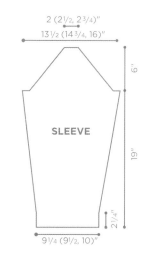

2 (2½, 2¾)"

13½ (14¾, 16)"

6"

SLEEVE

19"

2½"

9¼ (9½, 10)"

# asymmetrical mock cable vest/pullover and hat

## OVERVIEW

Entire garment is worked from Chart(s) on pages 114–117; side seams are indicated for reference only, as garment is worked in-the-round to underarm. Work only the sts at each seam indicated for your size. When working from Charts, read all rnds from right to left; when working straight, read RS rows from right to left, WS rows from left to right. All shaping is shown on the Chart(s).

## SPECIAL TECHNIQUE
**Mock Cables:** see Chart Key

## hat

Cast on 48 sts. Pm on RH needle for beg of round. Join, being careful not to twist sts. Beg 1x1 Rib, p1; work 2 rnds even.

**Establish Pattern:** Work 26 sts from Woman's Front Chart as indicated for Hat Front, beg Row 1, pm for side seam, purl to end of rnd (Rev St st). Cont as est, work even through Rnd 16 of Chart. Beg working back and forth in rows.

### Shape Front Crown

Row 17: (RS) P2tog, work 22 sts from Chart, p2tog, turn, leaving Back sts on hold at other side of needle.

---

*There are 4 sizes given; number corresponding to Child's size appears in < > before numbers for 3 Woman's sizes—if only one number is given, it corresponds to all sizes.*

### SIZES
**vest/pullover**
<Child's Small 2T–4T>; Woman's Small (Medium, Large)

**hat**
One size fits all.

Woman's vest shown in Small.

### KNITTED MEASUREMENTS
**Chest:** <28>; 33 ½ (36, 38 ½)"
**Length:** <14 ½>; 25 ¼"
**Sleeve at upper arm:** <12">; 16 ½ (18, 19)"
**Hat around crown:** 15 ½" (very stretchy)

### YARN
Rowan "Polar" (60% wool/30% alpaca/10% acrylic), bulky singles
<3 balls (3.5oz/100g; 109yds/100m) 650 smirk (lavender)>; 4 (5, 5) balls 640 stony (taupe)
Add <1>; 3 balls for sleeves
1 ball for Hat

### NEEDLES/TOOLS
US 11 (8mm) <24">; 24 (24, 32)" long circular for pullover/vest, 12" long for Hat, or size to match gauge
Stitch markers
Cable needle (cn)
Stitch holders/spare circular needle
Crochet hook J-10 (6mm)

### GAUGE
12 sts and 16 rows = 4" in Rev St st in-the-round, you can measure across lower back of Hat.

Always check and MATCH gauge for best fit.

**Row 18:** Work even from Chart.

Cont as est, dec 1 st each side EOR twice more, then every row 6 times as foll: If sts are purl sts, P2tog; if sts are knit sts, work a right-slanting dec at RH side, a left-slanting dec at LH side. The incs at the center of the cable will compensate for 8 of the decs—13 sts. Bind off.

**Shape Back Crown:** Join yarn at beg of RS row; cont in Rev St st, dec 1 st each side this row, then EOR 5 times more, bind off rem 10 sts.

Sew seams along crown shaping and graft sts at top tog, easing in extra Front sts to allow cable to fold.

## vest/pullover
### BODY
Cast on <84>; 100 (108, 116) sts. Pm on RH needle for beg of round. Join, being careful not to twist sts. Beg Chart, working only the sts indicated for your size at each side seam. On last rnd before underarm bind off, work to <2>; 2 (4, 6) sts before marker for beg of rnd.

Dividing Rnd—Rnd <34>; Rnd 62 on Chart: As indicated on Chart, bind off <4>; 4 (8, 12) sts for underarm, work across <38>; 46 (46, 46) sts for Front, bind off <4>; 4 (8, 12) sts for underarm, work across <38>; 46 (46, 46) sts for Back; place Back sts on holder.

### FRONT
Working on Front sts only, cont from chart, working armhole and neck shaping as indicated.

### BACK
Cont from chart, working armhole and neck shaping as indicated.

### SLEEVES
(optional)

### LEFT SLEEVE
With RS facing, beg at left Front armhole edge, where shaping ends, pick up and knit <26>; 40 sts along straight edge of armhole, ending at left Back where shaping ended. Beg Rev St st.

**Shape Sleeve Cap:** (RS) Inc 1 st each side EOR <3>; 3 times.

Cast on <2>; 2 (4, 6) sts at beg of next 2 rows to match underarm shaping—<36>; 50 (54, 58) sts.

**Shape Sleeve:** Dec 1 st each side every 6th row <4>; 10 times—<28>; 30 (34, 38) sts.

Work even until sleeve measures <13">; 19" from pick up row or desired length. Bind off.

### RIGHT SLEEVE
Cast on and shape as for Left Sleeve, working in Irish Moss (Double Seed) st (see Chart Back, RH side) instead of Rev St St.

### FINISHING
Graft shoulder seams.

With RS facing, using crochet hook, beg at side seam, work single crochet into each st around cast on edge; fasten off.

**Vest—Armhole Edging:** With RS facing, using crochet hook, beg at underarm, work single crochet into each st around armhole edge.

**Pullover:** Set in Sleeves; sew Sleeve seam.

BACK AND FRONT WOMAN'S

5½" 3½" 4¼"

1¼"

6¼"

8¾"

25¼'

15¼"

33½ (36, 38½)"

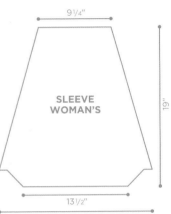

9¼"

SLEEVE WOMAN'S

19"

13½"

16½ (18, 19)"

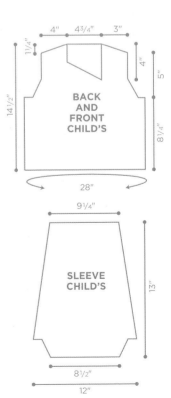

BACK AND FRONT CHILD'S

4" 4¾" 3"

1¼"

4"

5"

14½"

8¼"

28"

9¼"

SLEEVE CHILD'S

13'

8½"

12"

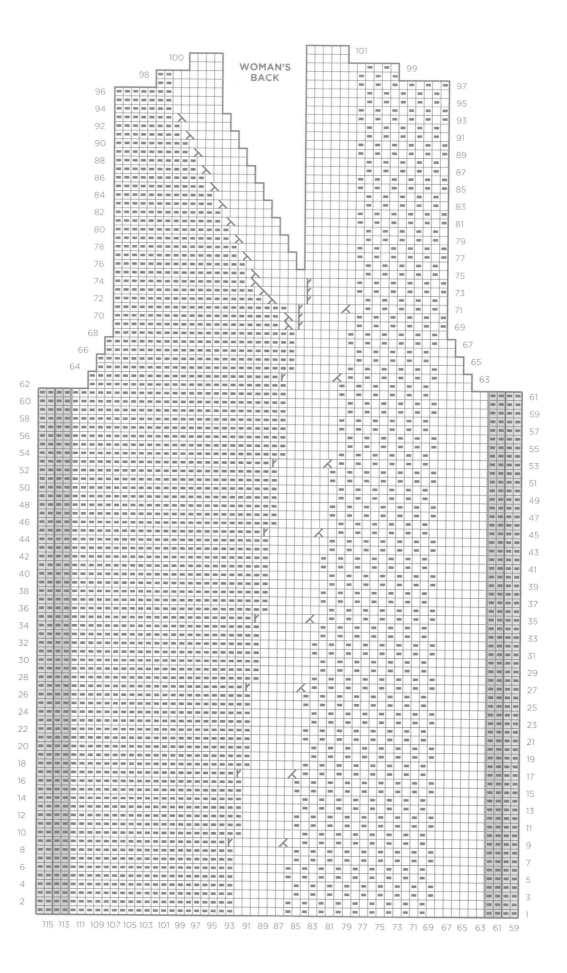

WOMAN'S
BACK

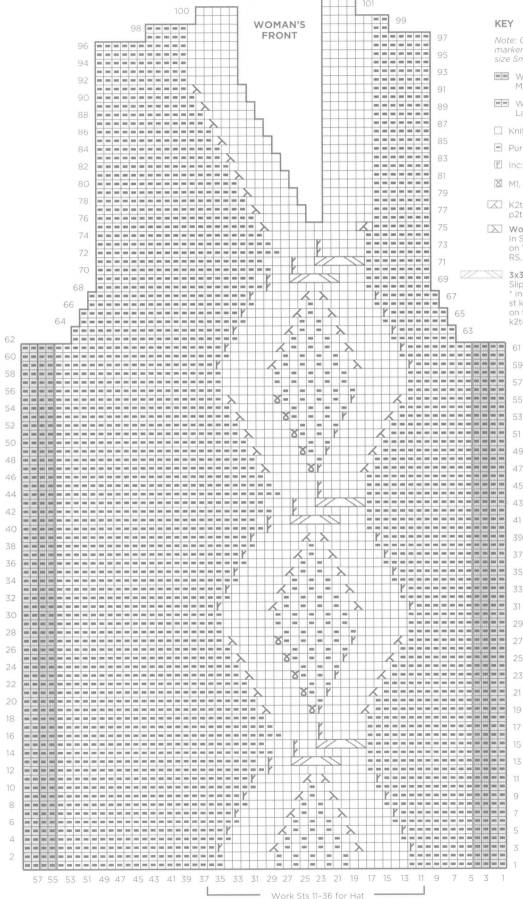

**WOMAN'S FRONT**

Work Sts 11–36 for Hat

**KEY**

*Note: Green lines indicate where markers are placed for side seams, size Small, while working in-the-round.*

⊞⊞ Work these sts for Sizes Medium and Large.

⊟⊟ Work these sts for Size Large only.

☐ Knit on RS, purl on WS.

⊟ Purl on RS, knit on WS.

⧄ Inc: K-f/b or p-f/b in pattern.

⊠ M1, k1

⧄ K2tog on RS, p2tog on WS.

⧄ Work in patt: In St st—Ssk on RS, p2tog-tbl on WS; In Rev St st—p2tog on RS, k2tog on WS.

⬚ 3x3 Mock Cable Cross [dec]: Slip 3 sts to cn, hold to back, * insert RH needle tip into next st knitwise, then through the st on the RH end of the cn and k2tog; rep from * twice—3 sts dec.

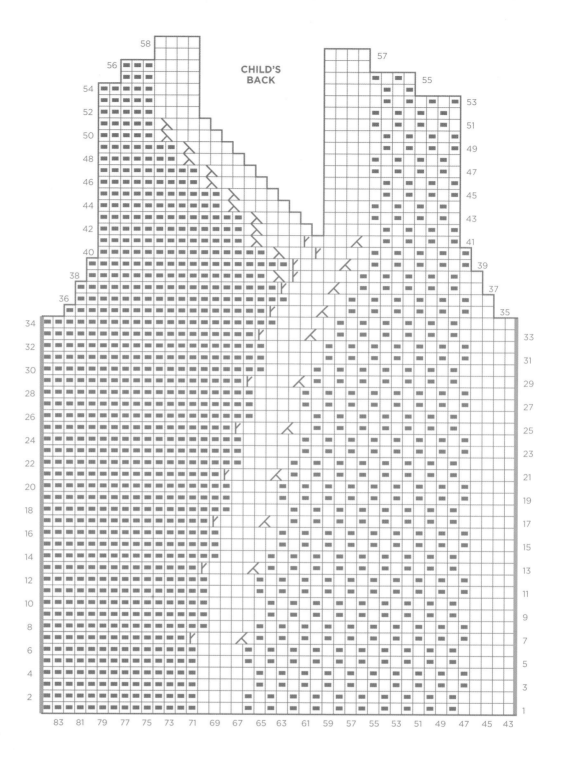

CHILD'S
BACK

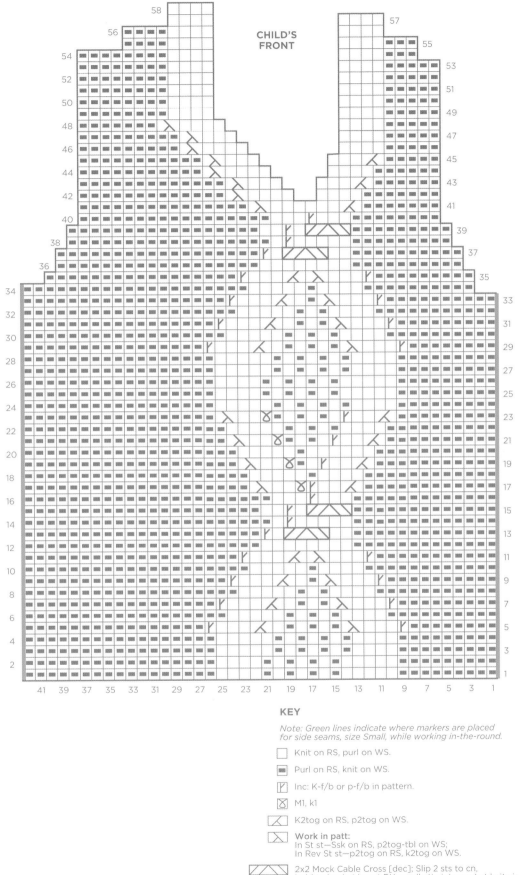

**CHILD'S FRONT**

**KEY**

*Note: Green lines indicate where markers are placed for side seams, size Small, while working in-the-round.*

☐ Knit on RS, purl on WS.

▦ Purl on RS, knit on WS.

Ⲩ Inc: K-f/b or p-f/b in pattern.

⊠ M1, k1

⟋ K2tog on RS, p2tog on WS.

**Work in patt:**
In St st—Ssk on RS, p2tog-tbl on WS;
In Rev St st—p2tog on RS, k2tog on WS.

2x2 Mock Cable Cross [dec]; Slip 2 sts to cn,
hold to back, * insert RH needle tip into next st knitwise,
then through the st on the RH end of the cn and k2tog;
rep from * once—2 sts dec.

# braided neckpiece

**SIZE**
One size

**KNITTED MEASUREMENTS**
Each piece is 8" wide and 24" long from center back neck

**YARN**
Karabella Yarns "Super Cashmere" (100% cashmere), bulky of 5 cabled 2-ply strands

**NEEDLES/TOOLS**
3 balls (1.75oz/50g; 81yd/75m) in 76 ivory
Size US 11 (9mm) 24" long circular, or size to match gauge (project is worked in rows but circular needles needed for flexibilty and length)
5 Stitch holders or waste yarn

**GAUGE**
12 sts and 16 rows = 4" in St st
Always check and MATCH gauge for best fit.

**OVERVIEW**

This scarf is constructed in two pieces. The first is worked from side-to-side (cast on for the length) In Rev St st and has 4 slits, which will provide a base for other side to weave through. The second piece is picked up along the side edge of the first (at what will be center Back neck), then worked to Front neck; there it is separated into angled straps that are woven through the first piece, then rejoined so the two pieces are permanently connected at front neck. All outside edges have Garter st or Rib to prevent rolling.

**PIECE 1**

Using long-tail cast-on method, cast on 74 sts.

Row 1: (RS) Work across in 1x1 Rib.

Row 2: Knit.

Row 3: Establish Pattern: K2 (garter st edging for lower edge of scarf), purl to end (St st).

Row 4: Knit.

Row 5: K2, purl to end.

Row 6: K30, bind off 17 sts, knit to end.

Row 7: K2, p25, using single cast-on method, cast on 17 sts over bound off sts, purl to end.

Rows 8–11: Work in patt as est, maintaining 2 sts in garter st at lower edge.

Rows 12–29: Rep Rows 6–11.

Row 30: (WS) Work across in 1x1 Rib.

Bind off in rib.

**PIECE 2**

With Rev St st side of Piece 1 facing, beg at upper edge (non-Garter st edge) pick up and knit 25 sts across the 30 rows.

**Next Row:** (WS) K2 (Garter st edge), purl to last 2 sts, k2 (Garter st edge).

**Next Row:** Knit.

Rep these 2 rows, working 2 sts each side in garter st, rem sts in St st, until piece measures 10", end with a WS row.

**Straps:** Cont in patt as est, work as foll:

**Rows 1 and 3:** (RS) K20; leaving rem 5 sts unworked, turn.

**Row 2 and all WS rows:** Purl to last 2 sts, k2.

**Rows 5 and 7:** K15; leaving rem sts unworked, turn.

**Rows 9 and 11:** K10, leaving rem sts unworked, turn.

**Row 13:** K5, turn.

Work in patt est on these 5 sts until strap measures 5½" from beg, end with WS row; cut yarn, place sts on holder.

**Remaining straps:** With RS facing, * join yarn to next group of 5 sts; work in St st until strap measures 5½" from where it began; cut yarn, place sts on holder. Rep from * 3 times, working last strap in patt as est, with garter st edge sts; place sts on holder but do not cut yarn.

Without twisting fabric to WS (RS of both pieces facing), bend piece 2 around to meet piece 1 and weave Straps through the slits in Piece 1 as foll:

First, third and fifth Straps go over, under, over, under, over; second and fourth straps go under, over, under, over, under.

Return all sts to needle in correct order, ready for RS row; knit across to join. Work even in patt as est, maintaining garter st edges, until piece measures 8½" from joining row, end with a RS row.

**Next 2 rows:** K2, work in 1x1 Rib to last 2 sts, k2.

Bind off in rib.

Weave in ends and block lightly with steam.

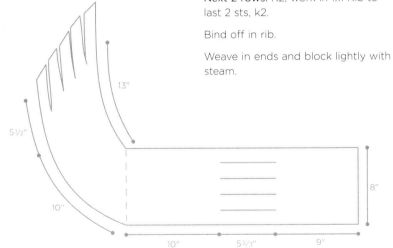

# cabled riding jacket

## OVERVIEW

Jacket is knit in one piece to armholes. There are 10 cables (5 pairs of opposing honeycomb-like cables) on Back and 5 cables on each Front (2 pairs and 1 single cable, which becomes a set at center Front, when jacket buttons). The lower body is shaped by decreasing the purl sts between cables—done alternately on the purl sts to the inside of the pairs (9 decs per round) or between the sets (10 decs per rnd). The wavy cables done by alternating direction of twist up each column transform at the waist to twist in same direction and more frequently, which draws the fabric in. Then the cables are skewed on the bias for the Front. The sleeves' bias cuffs match the bodice, while their honeycomb cables match the hem. The sizing is achieved by adding a purl st between cable pairs—be careful to follow chart rep for your size.

## BODY

Using long-tail cast-on method, cast on 213 (223, 233) sts.

**Establish Pattern (follow chart on page 123):** (WS) Beg at left Front, K4, p5, k6 (7, 8), [p5, k5, p5, k6 (7, 8)] 8 times, p5, k4.

**Row 2:** (RS) k1, p3, k5, [p6 (7, 8), k5, p5, k5] 8 times, p6 (7, 8), k5, p3, k1.

Cont as est, work Rows 3–72 of Chart, working buttonholes on right Front Band every 12 rows as shown. *Note: Waist begins on Row 60—pay attention to changes in direction and frequency of Cable twists.*

## SIZES
Small (Medium, Large)
**Shown in Small.**

## KNITTED MEASUREMENTS
**Chest:** 38 (40½, 43)" closed (1" overlap)

**Waist:** 29½ (32, 34½)" closed

**Hem:** 47½ (50, 52½)" closed

**Length:** 28½"

**Sleeve at upper arm:** 12½ (13½, 14½)"

## YARN
Mostly Merino "Fine Vermont Wool" (77% merino & corriedale wool/23% mohair), 2-ply worsted

13 (14, 15) in hanks (2oz/57g; 125yd/115m) in stone (olive)

## NEEDLES/TOOLS
US 8 (5mm) circular, at least 36" long for body, 12" long for cuff, or size to match gauge

Cable needle (cn)

Stitch markers

Stitch holders/spare circular needles

Tapestry needle

## NOTIONS
Twelve ½" post buttons*, matching thread, and sewing needle

## GAUGE
16 sts and 24 rows = 4" over St st.

16 sts and 24 rows = 3" over two 8-st reps of 5-st cables with 3 purl sts between, twisted every 4 rows.

16 sts and 24 rows = 3¼" over two 8-st reps of 5-st cables with 3 purl sts between, twisted every 6 rows.

Always check and MATCH gauge for best fit.

*I used carved wooden buttons made to look like woven leather.

## BODICE

Cont buttonholes as est [every 12 rows] 6 times more. Twist all cables every 6th row; the 5 cables on right Front—work as 5-st Right Cable, the 10 cables on Back—cont slant as for Row 72 of Chart; the 5 cables on left Front—work as 5-st Left Cable. Bias effect begins on Row 2.

**Row 1:** (WS) Foundation Row—K4, p5, [k3 (4, 5), p5, k3 (2, 1), inc (p-f/b) into next 0 (1, 2) sts, p5] twice, k1, pm for side seam; k2 (3, 4), [p5, k3, p5, k3 (4, 5)] 4 times, p5, k3, p5, k2 (3, 4), pm for side seam; k1, [p5, inc into next 0 (1, 2) sts, k3 (2, 1), p5, k3 (4, 5)] twice, p5, k4—165 (179, 193) sts; 42 (46, 50) sts each Front and 81 (87, 93) sts Back.

**Row 2:** K1, p2, pm, inc [k5, p3 (4, 5)] 4 times, k4, k2tog (1 st from cable, tog with purl st), sl m, p2 (3, 4), [k5, p3, k5, p 3 (4, 5)] 4 times, k5, p3, k5, p2 (3, 4), sl m, p1, ssk, k4, [p3 (4, 5), k5], 4 times, inc, pm, p2, k1. Cont to inc and dec, for bias effect on Fronts, every RS row as est, for a total of 37 times, maintaining Cable patt as est.

AT SAME TIME

**Shape Sides:** Inc 1 st at each side seam marker every 4th row 7 times, by working M1 between the dec and the marker.

**Shape Back:** Work shaping on Back by inc every 20th row 3 times as foll:

**Row 20:** First Increase Row—Inc 1 st on purl st in center of each of the 5 pairs of cables—5 sts inc.

**Row 40:** Second Increase Row—Inc between the 5 pairs of cables, but not at sides—4 sts inc.

**Row 60:** Third Increase Row—Work as Row 20—5 sts inc, a total of 14 sts inc across Back over 60 rows.

*Note: The third inc row will be after the armhole shaping.*

AT SAME TIME

**Dividing Row:** (RS) There are 188 (202, 216) sts; 49 (53, 57) sts each Front and 90 (96, 102) sts for Back.

**Row 42 (38, 36):** * Work as est to 3 (4, 5) sts before side marker; join new yarn, bind off 6 (8, 10) sts; rep from * once, work to end—46 (49, 52) sts each Front and 84 (88, 92) sts for Back.

**Shape Armhole:** (WS) Cont as est, work Fronts and Back separately; at each armhole edge, dec 1 st EOR 7 times.

*Note: For bias effect on Fronts, decs need to cont at armhole edge on RS rows; work the armhole shaping on WS rows. You will be dec every row for 14 rows at Front armholes, in order to shape armhole and keep fabric on bias—39 (42, 45) sts each Front and 70 (74, 78) sts Back. After Bodice Row 60, there will be 75 (79, 83) sts for Back.*

## Shape Front Neck

**Rows 76 and 77:** Bind off 4 sts at beg row, place 2 (0, 2) sts on holder (these are the beg of cable at bias edge that occurs for these sizes; you will graft them to the collar for a continuous look).

*Note: In order to shape neck, discontinue inc at each edge as est for bias effect (this will substitute for neck edge decs—8 sts each side before shoulder shaping, 3 during), while cont to dec at armhole edge for bias effect.*

Armhole measures 8½ (9, 9½)", 25 (30, 31) sts each Front.

## Shape Front Shoulders

**Row 92 (left Front) and Row 93 (right Front):** Dec 1 for bias, bind off 9 (10, 10) sts.

**Rows 94 and 95:** Dec 1 for bias, bind off 8 (9, 9) sts.

**Rows 96 and 97:** Dec 1 for bias, bind off 6 (8, 9) sts.

## Shape Back Shoulders and Neck

**Rows 92–97:** Bind off 9 (10, 10) sts beg next 2 rows, 9 (9, 10) sts beg next 2 rows, 8 (9, 9) sts beg of next 2 rows.

**Row 98:** Bind off rem 23 (23, 25) sts for neck.

## RIGHT CUFF

Work 5-st Right cables as for bodice, with fabric skewed right as foll:

Using long-tail cast-on method and smaller circular needle, cast on 48 (54, 60) sts. Pm on RH needle for beg of round. Join, being careful not to twist sts.

**Rnd 1:** [P3 (4, 5), k5] 6 times.

**Rnd 2:** [Inc (p-f/b), p1 (2, 3), k2tog, k4] 6 times.

Rep these 2 rnds, twisting cable every 6th rnd, beg Rnd 7.

**Shape Right Cuff:** When piece measures 6" from the beg, dec 6 sts evenly around by working Rnd 2, eliminating the inc for each rep—42 (48, 54) sts.

Work even in Cable patt for 2" more, inc (p-f/b) 6 sts between cables on last rnd—48 (54, 60); Cuff measures 8" from beg.

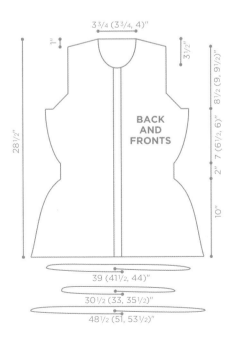

## LEFT CUFF

Work 5-st left cables as for Bodice, with fabric skewed left as foll:

Cast on as for right Cuff.

**Rnd 1:** [K5, p 3 (4, 5)] 6 times.

**Rnd 2:** [K4, ssk, p1 (2, 3), inc (p-f/b)] 6 times.

Rep these 2 rnds, twisting cable every 6th rnd, beg Rnd 7.

Shape left Cuff as for right Cuff—48 (54, 60) sts; cuff measures 8" from beg.

## SLEEVES

**Divide for Sleeve Seam:** (RS) Remove marker, sl 1 (2, 2) sts (this will be sleeve seam), p2 (2, 3), [k5, p 3 (4, 5)] 5 times, k5, inc 1 (0, 1) times, p0 (1, 1), turn—49 (54, 61) sts.

Cont in patt as est, knit the knits and purl the purls.

**Row 7:** (RS) Twist Cables as for Row 6 of Chart.

**Row 13:** Twist Cables as Row 12 of Chart, disregarding the decs between cables.

Work as est, twisting Cables every 6th row, for opposing honeycomb cables as for lower jacket;

AT SAME TIME

**Shape Sleeve:** Inc 1 st each side every 8th row 8 (9, 9) times—65 (72, 79) sts.

Work even until piece measures 21" from beg (13" from top cuff).

**Shape Sleeve Cap:** Bind off 3 (4, 5) sts beg of next 2 rows—59 (64, 69) sts.

Dec 1 st each side EOR 7 times—45 (50, 55) sts.

Work even for 1".

Dec 1 st each side EOR 6 times, then every row 7 times—19 (24, 29) sts. Bind off rem sts.

## FINISHING

Block lightly with steam. Sew shoulder seams, easing to match. Sew sleeve seams and set in sleeves. Sew buttons opposite buttonholes.

## RIGHT COLLAR

**Lining:** Cast on 3 sts.

**Row 1:** (WS) K3 (Rev St st).

**Row 2:** Inc (p-f/b), p1, inc.

Cont in Rev St st as est, inc 1 st each side EOR 3 times more—11 sts, end WS row; place sts on holder.

**Outer Piece:** Cast on 3 sts.

**Row 1:** (WS) P3.

**Row 2:** Inc (k-f/b), k1, inc.

**Row 3:** P5.

**Row 4:** Inc, k3, inc.

**Row 5:** K1, p5, k1.

**Row 6:** Inc (p-f/b), k5, inc.

**Row 7:** K2, p5, k2.

**Row 8:** Inc (p-f/b), p1, 5-st Right Cable, p1, inc.

**Row 9:** K3, p5, k3.

**Joining Row:** Take up Lining piece, inc, p10; using same yarn, work across Outer Piece: p3, k5, p2, inc—24 sts. Cont as est, keeping Lining in Rev St St, Outer Piece in Cable patt, turning cable every 6th row.

AT SAME TIME

Inc 1 st each side EOR 4 times more, then inc only at outer edge 3 (4, 5) times more, working outer edge sts in

Cable patt as foll: (RS) Work new sts as 5 knits, then 3 (4, 5) purls to match Cable patt on Bodice—35 (36, 37) sts.

Work even until right Collar measures approx 9 (9, 9½)" from beg; place sts on holder for center Back.

## LEFT COLLAR

Work as for right Collar, except on outer piece, reverse cable slant (Row 8, work 5-st Left Cable).

For Joining Row, work across sts of Outer Piece, then Lining; cont in patt as est, working Lining in Rev St st, Outer Piece in left slanting Cable patt; shape as for Right Collar.

Sew Lining to outer collar on center seam from cast on to joining row. Sew Lining along WS of neck edge. Sew cast on row of Outer Piece to neck bind off.

**Small and Large only:** Graft sts on holder to cast on row of Outer Piece, to give the illusion it is the beg of Cable column. Sew outer edge along RS of neck edge. Graft sts of Right Collar to Left Collar (on holders) at center Back neck with Kitchener st, unraveling or adding row(s) if necessary for best match fit along back neck.

**KEY**

Knit on RS, purl on WS.

Purl on RS, knit on WS.

No stitch

P2tog

**5-st Right Cable:** Sl 2 sts to cn, hold to back, k3, k2 from cn.

**5-st Left Cable:** Sl 3 sts to cn, hold to front, k2, k3 from cn.

**Buttonhole—Right Front only:** (RS) Yo, p2tog. (WS) Knit the yo.

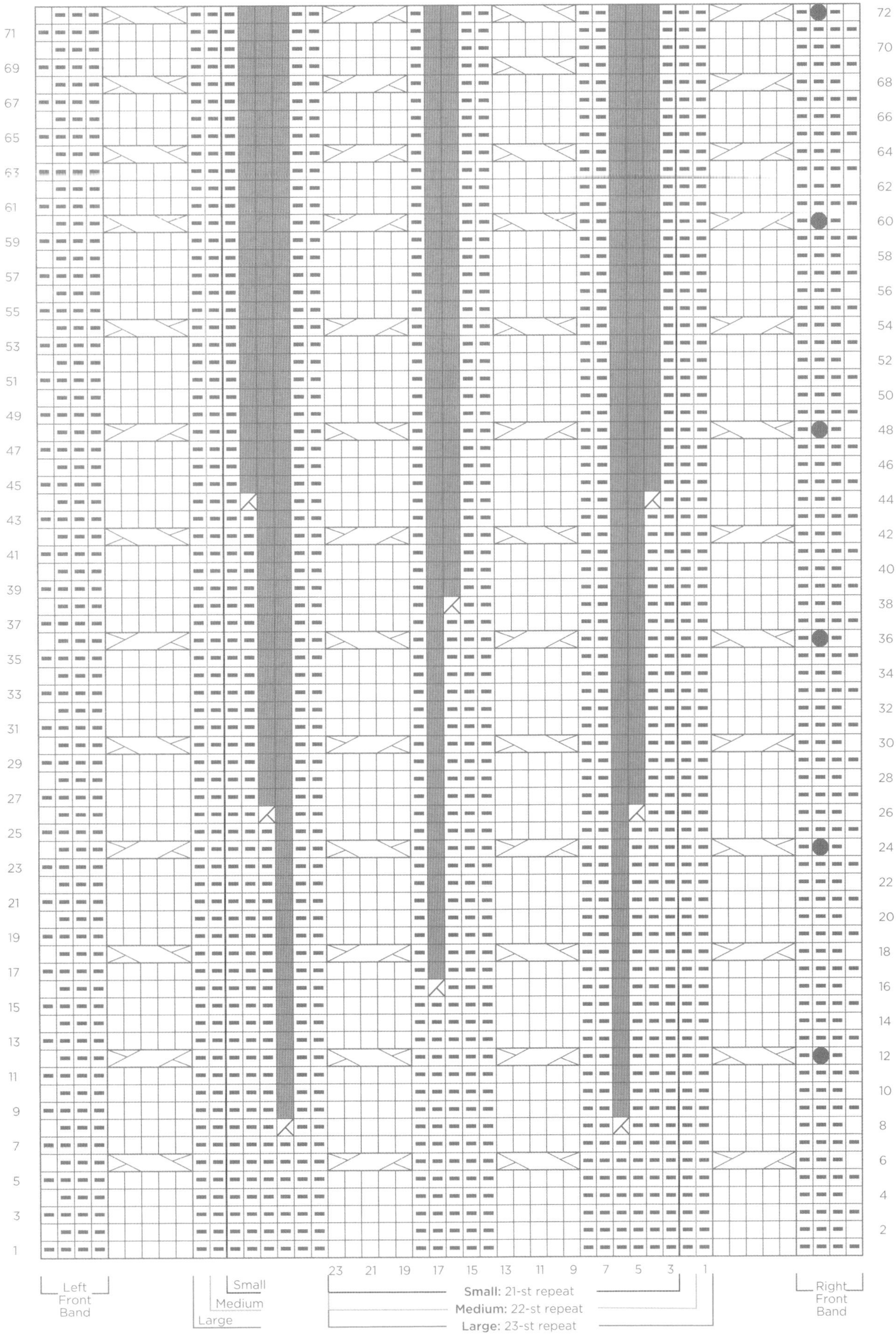
Left Front Band
Small
Medium
Large
Small: 21-st repeat
Medium: 22-st repeat
Large: 23-st repeat
Right Front Band

# CHAPTER 3

# WAVES

*Experiments in Color,*
*Pattern,*
*and Composition*

COLOR KNITTING TECHNIQUES, LIKE FASHIONS OR ANY OTHER TRENDS, EBB and flow in popularity as time goes by. The knitting patterns of the past three decades have predominantly featured three forms of colorwork: First, there have been stripes, from sporty to ethnic. At the same time, we've seen two-color stranded patterns, such as those found in Nordic ski sweaters, Shetland Fair Isle ganseys, Turkish socks, and Andean *chullos*. Then, there's intarsia: elaborate floral designs and "picture" sweaters derived from needlepoint designs, printed or woven textiles, and geometric or color-block concepts. While knitters continue to discover the glorious color artistry of Kaffe Fassett and the exquisite world Alice Starmore has built upon the Fair Isle tradition, techniques like mosaic, modular, domino, shadow, and freeform knitting are the current buzz. Knitters also like to sit back and let space-dyed or self-patterning yarn do all the work. Whatever the method, there is no denying the delight of seeing colors interplay and patterns evolve in your hands.

One of the best things I did for myself when I began this book project was to buy a lamp with a true-color bulb. I submitted small reels and knit swatches to its beams to see if the combinations resonated. Having grown up around tubes of Pthalo Blue, Cadmium Yellow, and the like, and discussions on Josef Albers (my parents met in art school), I learned early that we perceive color through light waves bouncing off objects, and the color we see is also relative to the environment and the nearby colors with which it interacts. A slight adjustment in one hue or value can take a combination from lackluster to thrilling. Color, like aroma, taste, or music, has the power to evoke emotion and leave a lasting impression. I make color choices by instinct, especially by association with memory, and within a certain palette I've developed through trial and error. I use gray, tan, and muddied, subdued hues to balance saturated, lively bursts of color. I'm fascinated by the ways various knit textures blend colors, especially at the blurred edges where colors meet. I like to shift the mood within a motif or piece by reversing light and dark values, cool and warm tones.

This chapter presents a sampling of colorwork projects in which I have tried to capture this kind of excitement. Many of the motifs reference the wave—light waves, ocean waves, the wavy chevrons of individual knit stitches. The color patterns are achieved, for the most part, with traditional techniques taken in new directions through novel construction or stitchwork.

## "fade-out" ribbed stole

This stole is just a ribbed tube. But it's a versatile layering piece—it can be a poncho, a hood, or even a skirt. I filled three horizontal bands in graduating values of the same hue, arranged from light to dark. In Shetland Fair Isle knitting, the background hue is often shifted in the same manner to integrate the space between pattern bands.

I selected a blue denim color to resemble jeans fading as the indigo dye is worn away, but you can use this piece as a canvas for your own color experiment.

>> See pattern on page 142.

## ibiza stripe shirt with shorts

Stripes are germane to flags and military insignia, but they've also been used to mark outcasts (jesters, convicts, sailors) for centuries. Michel Pastoureau, in *The Devil's Cloth: A History of Stripes and Striped Fabric*, writes about how the pattern was brandished by revolutionaries (such as George Washington) and transformed to chic.

The colors of these brash stripes are derived from my impression of Ibiza, an island in the Mediterranean off the coast of Spain. Now a place for disco raves in soapsuds, Ibiza holds a mythic place in my imagination. Before I was born, my grandmother and my parents lived there, quasi-beatniks seeking cheap living and an artistic scene. I know Ibiza only through my mother's flamenco guitar music, stories of disapproving matrons clad in black, and descriptions of the sun descending every evening in a burst of magenta that turns the whitewashed stucco churches to pastel pink.

>> See pattern on page 143.

## fair isle hooded capelet

Cloaks and mantels have been worn by both sexes, and all ages, throughout history. Their smaller, trendier cousins—capelets and ponchos—are all the rage now, and I developed this loop-d-loop design to meet that demand. The giant stitches are the perfect foil for a first attempt at Fair Isle stranding, as merely nine rounds creates a striking pattern (see left). They're just as chic worked up in a solid color (as above).

Although I have used red sparingly here, people remark that the young girl's capelet evokes Little Red Riding Hood. That cautionary tale, like the poncho itself, has been reinterpreted many times over the years (for book reviews and annotated tales, see www.surlalunefairytales.com/ridinghood). My favorite rendition of the story is James Thurber's modern version, in which the heroine pulls a gun from her basket and shoots the wolf. "It is not so easy to fool little girls nowadays," Thurber observes. Though, of course, I'm not literally in favor of people packing guns, I do promote girls taking care of themselves and believe this capelet suits such savvy girls of all ages.

>> *See pattern on page 146.*

## fair isle short-row pullover

In her *Book of Fair Isle Knitting*, Alice Starmore illustrates the paradox of the stranded colorwork that flourished in Fair Isle (one of the Shetland Islands) in the mid-nineteenth century: "a rich, exotic art with a wealth of pattern and color . . . yet produced by an uneducated people in remote isolation, harsh physical conditions, and extreme poverty." She explores the motifs' religious symbolism, their similarity to patterns on butter churn handles, and the mind's love of pattern play.

For my experiment here, I have taken two traditional pattern bands into a new millennium. With the use of short rows, the darker band appears to be crisscrossed around the body, like a ribbon being laced up. The lighter band gives the illusion of wedges of negative space, like the fabric underneath. The raised purl bumps of garter stitch in the more neutral colors help to distinguish the edges of each band. I love the subtle mixing achieved when garter stitch bumps of two colors overlap, as they do here in the trim.

*>> See pattern on page 148.*

## bias fair isle pullover and kerchief

Fair Isle sweaters traditionally use "waves" (chevrons) and "peaks" (diamonds) to transition between larger XOXO and small "peerie" pattern bands. Stacking the bands makes a fascinating puzzler. When the pattern is divided horizontally mid-band, we see a series of angled lines (V's) oriented in alternate directions; X-shapes are mirror images of V's that meet at their points, while O's are V's that meet at their legs. Broken apart vertically, the series yields a similar breakdown: V's are mirrored right and left.

Here, I've used waves to provide an undulating bridge from the large bands to the small. I've given high contrast to the large band in charcoal and cream, transitioning from it with a brown wave, then moving from warm red to violet to the cool blues of the peerie design. The small crisscross band is offset—its peak does not align with the peak of the wave—so it forces the eye to travel to the other motif in search of an echo. Placing a portion of the pattern on the bias makes the viewer see that part of the fabric as an entirety before analyzing its elements.

*>> See pattern on page 152.*

## child's geek spiral pullover

The Golden Section is a spiral growth pattern found in nature—in the swirl of seashells, the arrangement of flower petals, and the staggering of pinecone scales. It's based on Fibonacci's law, a numerical series in which each new number is the sum of the prior two. When expressed geometrically, ever-larger spirals spread outward from the center in a manner similar to the motif I've used for this sweater. An article in the Fall 2003 issue of *Interweave Knits* featured this phenomenon and the inspiring designs of several knitting mathematicians. For my venture into "geek" knitting, I selected the maplike colors of the desert, the jungle, and the vast ocean. By working the pattern only until the front is square, you can create a washcloth, hot pad, or one side of a pillow—or you can join several squares for a blanket.

>> See pattern on page 154.

## paisley carpetbag

Paisley is a traditional pattern in woven shawls from northern India, so named for the Scottish town the goods were exported through. I designed a scarf of crocheted paisley shapes for a *Vogue Knitting On-the-Go* book and wondered if such pieces could likewise be knit.

I swatched and swatched, at first producing amorphous shapes— blob, pipe, dolphin—then honing the proportion of the characteristic teardrop. I enlisted my friend Lisa for the challenge of producing enough to cover a large satchel. Lisa, an opera singer and milliner extraordinaire, took the task to heart. She referred to the paisley shapes as her "little babies," and claims that as each one evolved, she felt a maternal attachment to it; placing each completed paisley in a plastic bag with the others she would feel it had the best colorway or the most perfect teardrop, fetal shape. When Lisa reported the paisleys appeared in her dreams, I told her it was time to stop. I sewed her babies together myself, also appreciating the beauty of each.

>> See pattern on page 157.

## zip-off color-block yoke sweater

One of the most provocative images from my childhood was on a Rolling Stones album cover in my older brother's collection: a pair of jeans from waist to thigh, with a real, working zipper sewn down the fly—presumably Mick Jagger's. The zipper is a symbol of raciness, of the industrial age and easy access to sex (the Amish prohibit zippers along with automobiles). The zipper was first invented as a closure for shoes, which otherwise were fastened with multiple buttons or hooks and eyes. It took some streamlining and a shift in mores to make the sliding fastener acceptable on clothing.

For a few years, I toyed with the concept of a sweater pieced together with zippers, one that could be stripped away piece by piece, converting into an abbreviated, asymmetrical style. I was finally compelled to design it after being introduced to a garment industry trimming store that had aisles of zippers on shelves up to the ceiling, and desks of workers cutting zippers to order with custom pulls.

>> See pattern on page 160.

## slip-stitch intarsia kilt

The word *kilt* comes from "Celt," the same people whose descendents are famous for Aran and Fair Isle knitting. Historians believe the Celts wove highly patterned cloth—herringbone, checks, and plaids—even earlier than medieval times. Accounts from Roman legions describe them as wearing brightly colored striped and checkered garments, but the men are depicted as wearing pants then, not skirts (kilts). Queen Victoria was enthralled with the Scottish Highlanders who served as her kilt-clad security force, and it was in her era that the Tartan weave was romanticized and commercialized. From that time on, various clans registered their particular plaid. I associate the kilt not only with bagpipers, but with the short skirts of schoolgirls' uniforms and, of course, the elegant designs of Coco Chanel.

>> See pattern on page 162 (shown on man with Cowl with Drawstring [page 42]).

## large-scale herringbone pullover

When I started loop-d-loop, I looked for ways to place the familiar in an unfamiliar context. I hit upon the theme of making a traditional textile pattern (such as argyle or houndstooth) extremely out of scale and, often, asymmetrical. Not only do these blown-up patterns provide interesting inter-connecting shapes, but the giant areas make colorwork less fussy. I tried herringbone in several ways, imitating woven threads, brick-laying schemes, and the typical staggering of dark and light. I like to think of the V-like shapes as referencing the distinctive, rippled V pattern of stockinette stitch.

>> See pattern on page 164.

## reversible double-knit vest

My mother loves to browse in used book-stores and knows that when she comes across a seemingly rare knitting tome, it's her duty to score it for me. That's how I got my hands on *The Principles of Knitting* by June Hiatt. It contains some of the most detailed notes on complex techniques I've ever seen. I was intrigued by a section that explores double knitting: creating a two-faced, circular fabric while knitting flat. I have used the double-knitting technique for this lined vest, with an allover pattern of small holes.

I derived the random, piplike holes and also the crimson colors from one of my most vivid early childhood memories. Seeing an apple in a bowl on top of the refrigerator, I demanded that my mother give it to me. "No, not apple," she told me. "Apple!" I wailed. Finally, she gave in. She took the fruit down and started to peel it. "This is a pomegranate," she explained as she excised the pips and let me eat some of the tiny, juicy morsels. This was unexpected, so different from the creamy flesh of an apple. Now, I call up that experience whenever I feel jaded or lack drive. I remind myself that I could get something better than I hoped for.

>> See pattern on page 166.

# "fade-out" ribbed stole

**SIZES**
Small/Medium
(Large/X-large)
**Shown in Small/Medium.**

**KNITTED
MEASUREMENTS**
Circumference, stretched
40 (46)"; 15" tall stretched

**YARN**
Needful Yarns/King "Extra"
(100% merino), worsted; 8
cabled, 2-ply strands
2 (3) balls (1.75oz/50g;
128yd/117m) each in 1863
light blue (A), 1694 medium
blue (B), and 1668 dark
blue (C)
Waste yarn

**NEEDLES/TOOLS**
US 8 (5mm) 24" long circu-
lar, or size to match gauge
Tapestry needle

**GAUGE**
18 sts and 32 rounds = 4" in
1x1 Rib, measured stretched.
Always check and MATCH
gauge for best fit.

Work Tubular cast-on as follows:
Using waste yarn, cast on 90 (104)
sts using single cast-on. Cut yarn.

**Set-up Row:** With A, *wyib k1, yo
(wrap yarn over RH needle from back
to front; this yarn over will be slipped
on the next rnd and will become the
base for the purl sts); rep from * to
end of row, being careful not to lose
the final yo—180 (208) sts.

**Rnd 1:** Join by working into the first
st of the last row; knit every other st,
slipping what will become the purl st
as foll: * K1, wyif sl the yo purlwise,
yb; rep from * around.

**Rnd 2:** Purl every other st (the yo's)
and slip every other st as foll: * Wyib,
sl 1, yf, p1; rep from * around.

Rep the last 2 rnds once more.

Beg 1x1 Rib, and after a few rnds
remove waste yarn. Cont with A,
work even until piece measures 5"
from beg (measure stretched, as
relaxed will look like 6"; stretching
diminishes length). Join B; work even
in Rib for 5". Join C; work even in Rib
for 5". Bind off loosely in Rib. Or, for a
more challenging but neater edge,
work Tubular bind-off as foll:

Thread tapestry needle with strand of
yarn 3 times longer than measurement of piece to be bound off. Hold
sts of final row on circular needle. Slip
sts off 4 at a time, after they are
worked, pulling working yarn to correct tension (not ruffled; not too
tight). *Insert tapestry needle through
first st from back to front, into 2nd st
from front to back, into first st from
front to back, into 3rd st from back to
front, into 2nd st from back to front,
into 4th st from front to back, into 3rd
st from front to back, into 5th st from
back to front, into 4th st from back to
front; cont in this manner, working 4
sts at a time, rep from *; fasten off.

# ibiza stripe shirt with shorts

## OVERVIEW

Shirt is worked from side to side in one piece. Slip st selvedge is used to keep raw edges and seams clean. Sizing is done by adding rows to the body between sleeve shaping and neck shaping, but to streamline the pattern, the extra rows for larger sizes are inserted, but not indicated by change in row number. *Note: Numbers in < > refer to cropped version; where there is only one set of numbers, it refers to both styles.*

Shorts are worked in 2 pieces, one for each side hip/leg, from waistband down. They are sewn tog at Front and Back crotch. There is shaping at Front and Back crotch seams, and in the center of each piece for hip. The Left Hip/Leg piece has Front crotch at beg of RS rows and Back crotch at end of RS rows, whereas the Right Hip/Leg piece has Back crotch shaping at beg of RS rows and Front crotch shaping at end of RS rows.

## SIZES

Small (Medium, Large)
*Note that fabric is very stretchy when choosing size.*
**Shirt shown in Small, long style, shorts in Small.**

## KNITTED MEASUREMENTS

**Chest:** 30 (34½, 39)"
**Length:** <14 (14¼, 14½)>"; 22¼ (22½, 22¾)"
**Sleeve at upper arm:** 17 (17¾, 18½)"
**Waist:** 28½ (31½, 34½)"

**Hip:** 37½ (40½, 43½)"

## YARN

### shirt
Cascade "Pima Silk" (85% pima cotton/15% silk), 4-ply light worsted (use double strand)
<1> 2 skeins (1.75oz/50g; 109y/100m) each in 8374 apple green (A) and 8437 mint (C)
Cascade "Pima Tencel" (50% pima cotton/50% tencel), 4-ply light worsted (use double strand)

<1> 2 skeins (1.75oz/50g; 109y/100m) each in 7779 black (B), 5140 rose (D), and 5136 blush (E)

### shorts
Cascade "Pima Tencel"
4 (5, 5) skeins in 7779 black (MC)
Cascade "Pima Silk"
1 skein in 8437 mint (CC) (or any CC from Ibiza shirt)
Waste yarn

## NEEDLES/TOOLS

### shirt
US 13 (9mm) 32" long circular, or size to match gauge
Stitch holders
Tapestry needle

### shorts
US 5 (3.75mm) needles, or size to match gauge
US 5 (3.75mm) dpns or circular for I-cord trim
US 3 (3.25mm) needles

US 7 (4.5mm) needles
Stitch markers

## GAUGE

### shirt
10 sts and 14 rows = 4" in St st, using 2 strands held together

### shorts
22 sts and 28 rows = 4" in St st using US 5 (3.75mm) needles
Always check and MATCH gauge for best fit.

## shirt

**Stripe Pattern:** Using 2 strands held tog, work 8 rows using A, 1 row B, 2 rows A, 4 rows C, 3 rows B, 1 row D, 2 rows A, 5 rows C, 1 row D, 1 row E, 12 (14, 16) rows D, 2 (4, 4) rows B, 4 (4, 6) rows E, 4 rows A, 9 rows B, 3 rows C, 7 rows D, 2 rows A, 2 rows C, 1 row A, 10 (12, 14) rows E, 3 (5, 7) rows B, 10 rows A, 1 row D, 6 rows B, 8 rows C, 6 rows D.

### LEFT SLEEVE

Using long-tail cast-on method and 2 strands of A, loosely cast on 32 (34, 36) sts.

**Row 1:** (WS) Sl 1, knit to end.

**Row 2:** Sl 1, knit to end—2 rows of Garter st for trim.

**Rows 3–19:** Beg St st; maintaining sl st selvedge, work even in Stripe patt—piece measures 5½" from beg.

**Shape Underarm:** Cont as est in St st and Stripe patt, work as foll:

**Row 20:** (RS) Sl 1, inc (k-f/b), knit across to last 2 sts, inc, k1.

**Row 21:** Sl 1, purl to end.

**Rows 22–31:** Repeat Rows 20 and 21—44 (46, 48) sts.

### Shape Sides

**Row 32:** Using single cast-on method, cast on <13>; 34 sts, knit to end.

**Row 33:** Cast on <13>; 34 sts, purl to end—<70 (72, 74)>; 112 (114, 116) sts.

**Rows 34–43:** Work even in St st and Stripe patt;

**For Medium:** work 4 additional rows;

**For Large:** work 8 additional rows.

### Divide for Back Neck

**Row 44:** (RS) Work <35 (36, 37)>; 56 (57, 58) sts, turn. Leave rem sts on holder, or other side of circular needle,

for Front. (Make a note of last row of Stripe patt worked.)

**Rows 45–76:** Work even as est—9". Cut yarn, place sts on spare needle.

### FRONT NECK

With RS facing, join yarn at neck edge (middle of piece); work <35 (36, 37)>; 56 (57, 58) sts on hold for Front, beg Stripe patt at appropriate row.

**Row 44:** (RS) Sl 1, k2tog, knit to end.

**Row 45:** Sl 1, purl to end.

**Rows 46–55:** Rep Rows 44 and 45—<29 (30, 31)>; 50 (51, 52) sts.

**Rows 56 and 57:** Work even.

**Row 58:** Bind off 5 sts from neck edge for "keyhole".

**Row 59:** Sl 1, purl to end; cast on 5 sts over bound off sts of previous row.

**Rows 60–63:** Work even.

**Row 64:** Inc, knit to end.

**Row 65:** Sl 1, purl to end.

**Rows 66–75:** Cont to inc at neck edge EOR for a total of 6 times—<35 (36, 37)>; 56 (57, 58) sts.

**Row 76:** Sl 1, knit to end.

Joining Row

**Row 77:** Purl across Front sts, then cont across sts on spare needle for Back—<70 (72, 74)>; 112 (114, 116) sts.

**Rows 78–87:** Work even.

**For Medium:** work 4 additional rows;

**For Large:** work 8 additional rows.

### Shape Sides

**Rows 88 and 89:** Bind off <13>; 34 sts, work to end.

### Shape Underarm

**Row 90:** Sl 1, k2tog, knit to last 3 sts, ssk, k1.

**Row 91:** Sl 1 purl to end.

**Rows 92–101:** Rep rows 90 and 91.

### RIGHT SLEEVE

**Rows 101–116:** Work even.

**Row 117:** Sl 1, knit to end—Garter st trim.

**Row 118:** Sl 1, knit to end.

Bind off.

Weave in ends. Block lightly. Sew sleeve seam; sew side seams, leaving <0>; 3½" open at lower edge for side vents.

## shorts
### LEFT HIP/LEG

**Waistband Casing:** Using waste yarn and US 5 needles, cast on 78 (86, 94) sts. Beg St st; work even for 2 rows. Change CC and US 3 needles; work even for 1". Cont with CC, change to US 7 needles; work even for 2 rows, (this looser section of fabric will form turning rows of waistband, and will appear at the top of the Shorts). Change to MC and US 5 needles; cont in St st, work even for 1".

**Waistband Casing:** (RS) Fold waistband along the turning rows and work as foll: Insert RH needle knitwise into first st, then into the first purl loop from the first row of CC after the scrap yarn, k2tog; cont to work each st tog with a st from the first CC row across. Purl 1 row.

**Row 1:** (RS) K37 (41, 45), pm for hip, k41 (45, 49). *Note: Side hip marked here is not centered; there are more sts for Back, fewer for Front.* Cut and unravel scrap yarn.

### CROTCH AND HIPS

Cont in St st, using MC and size 5 needles, work shaping as foll:

**Shape Front Crotch:** At beg of RS rows, inc 1 st every 8th row 6 times as foll: K1 for selvedge, inc (k-f/b), work to end.

Cont as est until piece measures 7 ¾" after waistband, end with RS Row 53.

(WS) Using single cast-on method, cast on 3 sts at end of row.

(RS) Work cast on sts in patt est at beg of row, work to end.

Cont in this manner, cast on 4 sts EOR twice—this will take 6 rows; 17 new sts for Front crotch, 6 incs and 11 sts cast on.

AT SAME TIME

**Shape Hips:** Inc 1 st each side of marker every 4th row 5 times as foll:

Knit into front and back loop of st before marker, slip marker (sl m), knit into front and back loop of st after marker—2 sts inc, 1 at each side marker; 10 sts total inc each side of marker.

AT SAME TIME

**Shape Back Crotch:** At end of RS rows, inc 1 st every 6th row 8 times as foll: Work to last 2 sts, inc, k1 for selvedge. Cont as est until piece measures 7 ½" from waistband casing, end WS Row 52.

(RS) Using single cast-on method, cast on 2 sts at end of row.

(WS) Work cast on sts in patt est at beg of row, work to end.

Cont in this manner, cast on 2 sts EOR once, 4 sts once, then 5 sts once—

this will take 8 rows; 21 new sts for Back crotch, 8 incs and 13 sts cast on.

After all shaping—126 (134, 142) sts.

Work even until piece measures 10 ½" after waistband, end with a RS row.

Change to CC; purl 1 row. Do not cut yarn or bind off.

**I-Cord Trim:** (RS) Cont with CC, cast on 3 sts at beg of row for I-cord. Using dpn, [k2, sl 1, k1 (st from last row of leg), pass the sl st over the knit st; strand yarn across WS of work without turning]; * rep between brackets twice, then k2, sl 1, k2tog [2 sts from last row of leg], pass the sl st over the dec st; strand yarn across WS of work without turning. Rep from * across, working 4 sts of Leg tog with I-cord every 3 rows. Bind off 3 I-cord sts.

### RIGHT HIP/LEG

Work as for Left Hip/Leg, reversing all shaping; pm for hip shaping on RS row as foll: K41 (45, 49), pm, k37 (41, 45). Shape Back crotch at beg of RS rows, Front crotch at end of RS rows.

### FINISHING

**I-cord trim:** Using CC and dpn, work a piece of I-cord approx 38 (41, 44)" long to put through waistband casing as foll: Cast on 3 sts, k3, * without turning, slide sts to other needle tip and k3 on RS again, rep from *.

Fold each piece and sew leg seam from lower edge to crotch. Sew I-cord seam.

Place the 2 pieces together; leaving the waistband casing open, sew Back crotch of left piece to Back crotch of right piece; sew Front crotch.

Insert drawstring through casing, then sew Back waistband seam; sew Front waistband seam, leaving ¼" open at Front for drawstring.

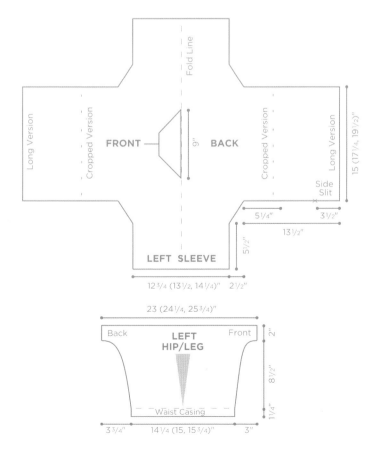

# fair isle hooded capelet

**SIZES**

<Child's Medium 4–8 year>; Woman's One Size fits most

**KNITTED MEASUREMENTS**

**Hem circumference:** <32">; 42½"

**Length to shoulder:** <14">; 16"

**YARN**

Rowan "Big Wool" (100% merino), 2-ply super bulky

**Solid color version:** <3>; 3 balls (3.5oz/100g; 87yd/80m) MC; Woman's shown in 022 swish (aqua)

**Fair Isle version:** <2>; 3 balls MC <019 smudge (gray)>; 027 best brown

1 ball each of 3 CCs <027, 028 bohemian (red), and 021 ice blue>; 028, 019 and 021

*Note: If making both Woman's and Child's, there will be enough MC left for 1 CC on each, and 1 ball of the other 2 CC colors will be enough for both garments.*

**NEEDLES/TOOLS**

<US 19 (15mm) 24" long circular>; US 36 (20mm) 24–36" long circular, or size to match gauge (US 36 47" length is more widely available, you can stretch excess length of tube out between sts)

Stitch marker

Tapestry needle

**GAUGE**

<8 sts and 11 rows/rnds>; 6 sts and 9 rows/rnds = 4" in St st using <smaller>; larger needle

Always check and MATCH gauge for best fit.

## OVERVIEW

Capelet is worked flat from the top of the Hood to shoulders, shaped with decorative yo incs, then joined at center Front neck and worked in-the-round to lower edge. When working yo's on large needles, be sure to wrap the yarn around the widest part of needle, and don't let sts slip down narrower needle tip. Also, let each stitch have fullest girth of the needle, in order to bind off loosely, so garment will not be constricting around lower edge.

## HOOD

Using appropriate needle size and MC, cast on 25 sts. Beg St st.

Row 1: (WS) Purl.

Row 2: K12, yo, k1, yo, k12.

Row 3 and all WS rows: Purl, working yo's as sts.

Row 4: K13, yo, k1, yo, k13.

Row 6: K14, yo, k1, yo, k14—31 sts.

Work even in St st until piece measures <11">; 13" from the beg, end with a WS row.

## BODY

Row 1: (RS) *K7, yo, k1, yo; rep from * twice more, end k7—37 sts.

Row 2 and all WS rows: Purl, working yo's as sts.

Row 3: K8, yo, k1, yo, k9, yo, k1, yo, k9, yo, k1, yo, k8—43 sts.

Row 5: K9, yo, k1, yo, k11, yo, k1, yo, k11, yo, k1, yo, k9—49 sts.

Row 7: Joining Row—K1, yo, k9, yo, k1, yo, k27, yo, k1, yo, k9, yo; pm, knit last st of row together with first st to join—54 sts.

Rnd 8 and all even-numbered rnds: Knit, working yo's as sts.

Rnd 9: K1, yo, k11, yo, k1, yo, k29, yo, k1, yo, k11, yo—60 sts.

Rnd 11: K1, yo, k59, yo—62 sts.

Rnd 13: K1, yo, k61, yo—64 sts.

## SOLID COLOR VERSION

Cont as est, work even in St st, using MC, until piece measures <9">; 10" from Joining Row.

**Optional:** Work 2 rnds in 1x1 Rib.

Bind off all sts loosely, knitwise.

## FAIR ISLE VERSION

Cont as est, work even in St st, using MC, until piece measures <4½">; 6" from Joining Row.

**Establish Fair Isle from Chart:** K16, pm for new beg of rnd (at side instead of center Front); beg Chart for your size, working in colors indicated, stranding non-working color loosely across WS of work.

Work Rnds 1–9 of Chart (work 16-st rep of Chart 4 times for each rnd), reading chart from right to left every rnd.

Change to St st using MC only; work even for 3 rnds.

Change to 1x1 Rib; work even for 2 rnds.

Bind off all sts loosely, knitwise.

## FINISHING

Block piece to measurements and to even out Fair Isle pattern, if used.

Weave in ends. Graft top of hood.

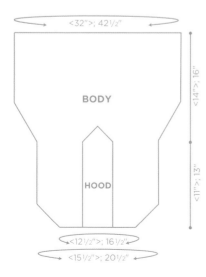

**WOMAN'S FAIR ISLE CHART**

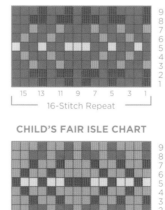

16-Stitch Repeat

**CHILD'S FAIR ISLE CHART**

16-Stitch Repeat

**KEY**

- Brown
- Gray
- Red
- Blue

# fair isle short-row pullover

## OVERVIEW

The diagonal bands of this sweater are created using Short Rows (see page 171). The Short Row segments skew the fabric to the bias, but after two segments the fabric levels out. The Back and Front are mirror images; there are 6 Short Row segments each on Front and Back. The Back has top-aligned Short Row segment from left, then bottom aligned Short Row from right, whereas the Front has top-aligned Short Row segment from right, then bottom aligned Short Row from left. All the Short Row segments occur in pattern Band 2; they are composed of 5 turns spaced 6 sts apart and are placed 11 sts past center Front st. Pattern Band 1 shifts alignment by ½ rep, as shown on Chart, each time to create interest because they are stacked at sides where Band 2 does not extend. The sleeves have no Short Rows, but match the order of segments at each side of Body, so the left and right Sleeves differ. To facilitate this, they are made the same length as the Body; then, as an average arm is about 3″ longer to wrist, sts are picked up and a trim is worked until Sleeve is an appropriate length. Top-aligned Short Row wedge will have contrast color loops in first row of Garter st band; duplicate st over the bumps with D, but leave CC sts visible on last row of Fair Isle.

## PATTERN STITCH
### Stripe Garter Trim

Beg with WS row, knit 2 rows A, 2 rows D, 2 rows A, 2 rows B; rep these 8 rows for Stripe Garter trim.

## BACK

Using long-tail cast-on method and A, cast on 97 (105, 113) sts. (WS) Beg

### SIZES
Small (Medium, Large)
**Shown in Small.**

### KNITTED MEASUREMENTS
**Chest:** 38½ (42, 45½)″
**Length:** 24 (24½, 25)
**Sleeve at upper arm:** 13 (14, 15)

### YARN
Jaeger "Matchmaker Merino Aran" (100% merino machine-washable), worsted

4 (5, 6) balls each (1.75oz/50g; 90yd/82m) in 639 granite gray (A), 766 soft camel (B), and 772 clover (lavender) (D)

3 (4, 5) balls each in 784 oatmeal (C), 769 prose (purple) (E), and 756 mulberry (F)

### NEEDLES/TOOLS
US 7 (4.5mm) circular, at least 24″ long, or size to match gauge

*Use circular needle so you can break yarn to start Short Rows in the right direction.*
Safety pins or hanging stitch markers
Tapestry needle

### GAUGE
20 sts and 24 rows = 4″ in Fair Isle patt from Chart
Always check and MATCH gauge for best fit.

Stripe Garter trim; work 8-row rep once, then knit 2 rows with A, end with a RS row.

*Note: Fair Isle patt is centered for each size, so all rows read the same from right to left as left to right, once the patt is est. The Row numbers given for Short Row segments are Chart Row numbers. RS and WS row designations change while working the Short Row segments; work Rev St st rows from RS or WS as appropriate.*

**Establish Fair Isle Pattern:** (WS) Beg Row 1, st 1 (13, 9) of Chart, work 16-st rep across, end st 1 (5, 9) of last rep. Work even as est through Row 13 of Chart.

* **Row 14:** (RS) First Short Row segment—Work as per Chart (using D, Rev St st), pm on center st—48 (52, 56) sts each side of marker.

**Row 15:** Cont from Chart, work across to center st, work 12 sts, wrap next st, turn (wrp-t).

**Rows 16, 18, 20 and 22:** Work as est to end.

**Rows 17, 19, 21 and 23:** Work across to 6 st rem before last wrap, wrp-t.

**Row 24:** Work as per Chart (using D, St st).

**Row 25:** Work as per Chart (using A, Rev St st) across all sts, working wraps tog with wrapped sts.

**Rows 26–41:** Work as per Chart, end WS row. Break yarn, DO NOT turn. Slide sts to opposite end of needle, ready to begin next Short Row segment with a WS row.

**Row 14:** (WS) Second Short Row segment—Work as for First Short Row segment, marking center st.

**Row 15:** Cont from Chart, work across to 12 sts before center st, wrp-t.

**Rows 16, 18, 20 and 22:** Work as est to end.

**Row 17, 19, 21 and 23:** Work across to 5 sts past last wrap, working wrap tog with wrapped st; wrp-t.

**Row 24:** Work as per Chart (using D, St st).

**Row 25:** Work as per Chart (using A, Rev St st).

**Rows 26–28:** Work as per Chart, end with a WS row.

**Rows 1–13:** Work as per Chart, end with a RS row. *

Break yarn, DO NOT turn. Slide sts to opposite end of needle, ready to begin next Short Row segment with a RS row.

Rep from * to * twice—6 Short Row segments total.

AT SAME TIME, when piece measures 15" along side edge (this will happen after 4 Short Row wedges, so fabric will be even), work armhole shaping while working rem Short Row segments.

## Shape Armholes

At each armhole edge, bind off 6 sts once, then dec 1 st EOR 6 times—73 (81, 89) sts.

After completing Short Row segments, work even from Chart, beg Row 14; work to end of Chart (Row 42), then rep Rows 1–42 until armhole measures 7 ½ (8, 8 ½)" from beg of shaping, end with a WS row.

## Shape Shoulders

Bind off 5 (6, 7) sts beg of next 4 rows, 4 sts beg of next 4 rows, then 3 sts beg of next 2 rows—31 (35, 39) sts rem for neck. Bind off neck sts.

## FRONT

Work as a mirror image of Back until armhole measures 6 ½ (7, 7 ½)" from beg of shaping—73 (81, 89) sts, end with a WS row; pm each side of center 15 (19, 23) sts.

**Shape Neck:** (RS) Cont as est, work across to marker; join a second ball of yarn and bind off center 15 (19, 23)

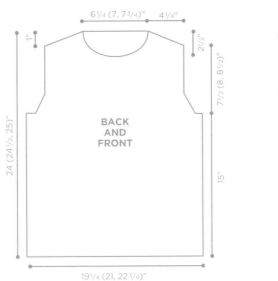

## FAIR ISLE CHART

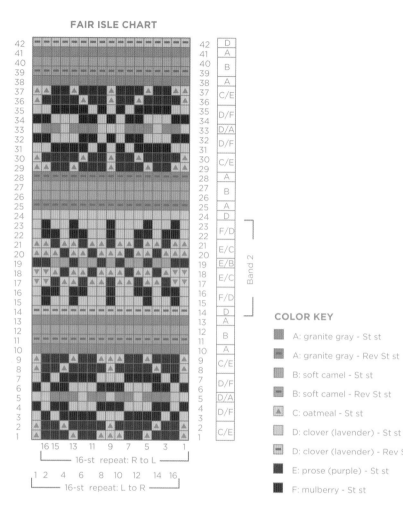

Band 2

16-st repeat: R to L
16 15  13  11  9  7  5  3  1

1  2  4  6  8  10  12  14  16
16-st repeat: L to R

| Row | Color |
|-----|-------|
| 42 | D |
| 41 | A |
| 40 | B |
| 39 | A |
| 38 | C/E |
| 37 | D/F |
| 36 | D/A |
| 35 | D/F |
| 34 | C/E |
| 33 | A |
| 32 | B |
| 31 | A |
| 30 | F/D |
| 29 | E/C |
| 28 | E/B |
| 27 | E/C |
| 26 | F/D |
| 25 | D |
| 24 | A |
| 23 | B |
| 22 | A |
| 21 | C/E |
| 20 | D/F |
| 19 | D/A |
| 18 | D/F |
| 17 | C/E |

### COLOR KEY

▦ A: granite gray - St st

▦ A: granite gray - Rev St st

▦ B: soft camel - St st

▦ B: soft camel - Rev St st

▲ C: oatmeal - St st

▦ D: clover (lavender) - St st

▦ D: clover (lavender) - Rev St st

■ E: prose (purple) - St st

■ F: mulberry - St st

sts; work to end. Working both sides at same time with a separate ball of yarn, at each neck edge, dec 1 st every row 4 times, then EOR 4 times as foll: At left neck edge, work dec as k2tog; at right neck edge, work dec as ssk.

AT SAME TIME, when armhole measures 7½ (8, 8½)" from beg of shaping, end with a WS row.

**Shape Shoulders:** as for Back.

### LEFT SLEEVE

Using long-tail cast-on method and A, cast on 49 sts. Using A, knit 1 (WS) row.

**Establish Fair Isle Pattern:** (RS) Beg Fair Isle Chart, Row 1, st 1; work 16-st rep across, end st 1 to center pattern.

* Work Rows 1–40; using A, purl 1 RS row; rep from * once, then work Rows 1–40 once more for patt;

AT SAME TIME, work even until piece measures 4 (3, 1)" from beg, end with a WS row.

**Shape Sleeve:** Inc 1 st each side this row, then every 6th row 6 (9, 12) times more, working new sts into pattern—63 (69, 75) sts. Work even until piece measures 15" from beg, end with a WS row at same place in sequence of Fair Isle bands as for left armhole shaping.

**Shape Sleeve Cap:** Bind off 6 sts at beg of next 2 rows—51 (57, 63) sts.

Dec 1 st each side EOR 12 times, then every row 5 (8, 11) times—17 sts. Bind off rem sts.

### CUFF

With RS facing, using A, pick up and knit 49 sts along cast on edge. Work in Stripe Garter Trim patt until Cuff measures 3" or desired length to wrist. Bind off all sts loosely.

### RIGHT SLEEVE

Work as for left Sleeve, working Fair Isle patt as foll:

**Establish Fair Isle Pattern:** Work as for left Sleeve through Row 13 of Chart; then work Rows 28–39, Rows 12–28, Rows 1–13, 28–39, then 12–28; cont with this sequence for rem of Sleeve, working shaping and Cuff as for left Sleeve.

AT SAME TIME, shape and work cuff as for left Sleeve.

### FINISHING

Graft left shoulder seam, using Kitchener st and dominant color of last row.

### COLLAR

With RS facing, beg at right Back shoulder using A, pick up and knit 74 (82, 90) sts around neck shaping. Work in Stripe Garter Trim for 2". Bind off. Graft right shoulder and side neck seam. Set in Sleeves being sure pattern bands match at side of body; sew side and sleeve seams.

# bias fair isle pullover and kerchief

## kerchief

To check gauge and become familiar with the Charted Fair Isle pattern and bias shaping, make the kerchief shown here.

Using A, cast on 3 sts; beg Fair Isle Chart, Row 1, Sts 6–8. Cont from Chart, work Rows 2–28, then rep Rows 1–28 for rem of piece for Fair Isle patt; and AT SAME TIME, work bias shaping starting on Row 2.

**Row 2:** (RS) Beg Bias Shaping—Inc 1 st at each side this row, then every RS row, working inc sts in patt from Chart, until 56 rows have been worked, end with a RS row.

**Row 57:** Bind off 1 st at beg of this row, then every WS row, while cont to inc at beg of RS rows for edge that fits along forehead. Cont as est until 62 rows have been worked.

**Row 63:** Bind off all sts.

**Ties:** (make 2) * With crochet hook (or fingers) attach F and G to corner of bottom edge and make a chain or braid, alternating between F and G, until Tie measures 12" from beg; cut yarn, pull through to secure and knot the end of the tie.

## pullover
### BACK AND FRONT BIAS HEMS
(both alike)

Using A, cast on 3 sts; beg Fair Isle Chart, Row 1, sts 6–8. Cont from Chart, work Rows 2–28, then rep Rows 1–28 for rem of piece for Fair Isle patt; and AT SAME TIME, work bias shaping starting on Row 2.

**Row 2:** (RS) Establish Bias Shaping—Inc 1 st at each side this row, then every RS row, working inc sts in patt from Chart, until 68 rows have been worked.

**Row 69:** (WS) Bind off 1 st at beg of this row, then every WS row to form top edge, while cont to inc at beg of RS rows for lower edge, until Row 107 (121, 135) is completed.

**Row 108 (122, 136):** (RS) Bind off 1 st at beg of this row, then every RS row, while cont to dec 1 st at beg of WS rows, until 2 sts rem; k2tog, pull yarn through to secure.

## SIZES
Small (Medium, Large)
**Shown in Small.**

## KNITTED MEASUREMENTS
**Chest:** 38 ¾ (43 ½, 48)"
**Length:** 23 (24, 24 ½)"
**Sleeve at upper arm:** 14 ½ (15 ¾, 17)"

## YARN
Dale of Norway "Freestyle" (100% wool, machine washable), 4-ply worsted

4 (5, 6) balls (1.75oz/50g; 86yd/80m) in 3946 red (B)

3 (4, 5) balls each in 5533 lavender (A), 3172 brown (C), 0083 charcoal (D), and 2611 natural (E)

2 (2, 3) balls each in 5703 light blue (F) and 6135 turquoise (G)

Gauge Swatch Kerchief takes a small amount of each of the 7 colors.

## NEEDLES/TOOLS
US 7 (4.5mm) needles, or size to match gauge

Stitch markers
Tapestry needle

**For decorative trim:**
Crochet hook H/8 (5mm) —or—an additional tapestry needle—or—US 7 (4.5mm) 16" circular needle

## GAUGE
20 sts and 22 Rows = 4" in St st Fair Isle patt
Always check and MATCH gauge for best fit.

## BACK BODICE

Take up one Bias Hem piece; using A, pick up and knit 97 (109, 121) sts along top edge.

**Establish Pattern:** (WS) Beg Fair Isle Chart, Row 1, st 1; work 8 (9, 10) 12-st reps across, ending as shown on Chart to center patt. Cont as est from Chart, work even until piece measures 2 (2½, 2½)" from pick up, end with a WS row.

**Shape Armhole:** Dec 1 st each side EOR 6 times—85 (97, 109) sts.

Cont as est from Chart until armhole measures 7½ (8, 8½)" from beg of shaping, end with a WS row.

**Shape Shoulders and Neck:** Bind off 7 (8, 9) sts at beg next 4 rows, 4 (5, 6) sts beg of next 4 rows—41 (45, 53) sts rem for neck; bind off rem sts.

## FRONT BODICE

Take up rem Bias Hem piece; work as for Back until armhole measures approx 6½ (7, 7½)" from beg of shaping (this should be 8 rows from beg of shoulder shaping), end with a WS row; pm each side of center 29 (33, 41) sts for neck.

**Shape Neck and Shoulders:** Work across to marker; join a second ball of yarn, bind off center 29 (33, 41) sts; work to end.

Working each side separately, at each neck edge, dec 1 st EOR 6 times; and AT SAME TIME, when armhole measures same as back to shoulder shaping, end with a WS row.

**Shape Shoulder:** as for Back.

## SLEEVES

Using A, cast on 49 (55, 61) sts.

**Establish Pattern:** (WS) Beg Fair Isle Chart, Row 1, centering Fair Isle patt on sleeve. Cont as est from Chart, work 5 rows even, end with a WS row.

**Shape Sleeves:** Cont as est from Chart, inc 1 st each side this row, then every 6th row 12 times total, working increased sts in Fair Isle patt—73 (79, 85) sts. Work even until piece measures 18½" from beg, end with a WS row.

**Shape Sleeve Cap:** Dec 1 st each side EOR 6 times—61 (67, 73) sts. Bind off all sts.

## FINISHING

Block pieces lightly with steam; pull at Bias Hem edges to achieve most straight vertical line for side seam. Sew left shoulder seam.

**Collar:** With RS facing, beg at right Back neck using C, pick up and knit 41 (45, 53) sts along Back neck, 51 (55, 59) sts along Front neck—92 (100, 108) sts. Work Chart Rows 17–28 then Rows 1–7; bind off all sts loosely.

Sew right shoulder and Collar seam. Sew side and sleeve seams. Set in sleeves.

**Decorative Trim:** Work around Collar edge, lower edge of Sleeve, both edges of Bias Hem and around pick-up row of Bodice.

With RS facing, using crochet hook and 1 strand each of F and G held to the WS, work slip st into each st around, alternating colors. *Note: If you don't feel comfortable crocheting, you can achieve the same effect with one of these alternatives:*

1. With RS facing, using a circular needle and holding one strand each F and G to WS, loosely pick up and knit sts, alternating colors, in each st around the edges, then bind off picked-up sts by passing one over the next, without knitting them first.

2. With RS facing, thread one tapestry needle with F and a second with G; work chain stitch embroidery around all edges, alternating colors.

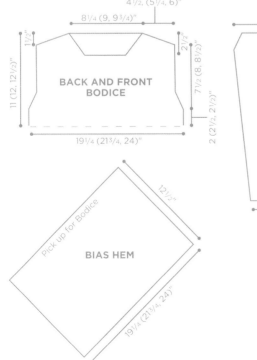

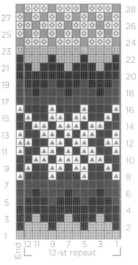

## FAIR ISLE CHART

**COLOR KEY**

Work in St st (knit on RS, purl on WS). Read RS rows from right to left; WS rows from left to right

A: lavender
B: red
C: brown
D: natural
E: charcoal
F: turquoise
G: light blue

12-st repeat

# child's geek spiral pullover

Back, Sleeves, and Hood are worked using main color (MC) in St st. Front is worked from the center out, in triangles of 4 contrast colors (CC), each picked up from the sides of the 2 previous triangles. Each time sts are picked up, the colors shift counterclockwise to create the swirl effect. As chenille yarn has little elasticity, it is important to bind off loosely. You may want to sew pieces together with wool or cotton yarn of matching colors.

**FRONT**

**SECTION 1—CENTER TRIANGLES**
Using A, cast on 1 st; beg Garter st.

Row 1 and all WS rows: Knit.

Row 2: (RS) Inc (k-f/b).

Row 4: Inc, inc.

Row 6: Inc, k2, inc.

Row 8: Bind off 6 sts—1A Triangle completed.

Using rem 3 CC, work as above—4 triangles.

**SECTION 2**
With RS of 1A facing, using D, pick up and knit 6 sts along bound off edge; beg Garter st.

Row 1 and all WS rows: Knit.

Row 2: (RS) Ssk, k2, k2tog.

Row 4: Ssk, k2tog.

Row 6: K2tog.

Row 8: Pull loop through rem st to secure.

Using rem 3 CC, work as above, using A on 1B; B on 1C; C on 1D.

Arrange pieces as shown on Front Diagram; sew 4 pieces tog to form a square as shown.

**SIZES**
Small 6–18 months
(Medium 2–4T, Large 4–6)
**Shown in Medium.**

**KNITTED MEASUREMENTS**
Chest: 24 (26, 28)"
Length: 13 (14, 15)"
Sleeve at upper arm: 9½ (10½, 11½)"

**YARN**
Crystal Palace "Cotton Chenille" (100% cotton), worsted weight chenille

5 (5, 6) hanks (1.75oz/50g; 98yd/90m) 7676 teal (MC)

1 hank each in 3417 khaki (A); 9008 light blue (B); 2342 lime green (C); and 4065 dk blue (D)

**NEEDLES/TOOLS**
US 6 (4.25mm) needles*, or size to match gauge
*Circular helps for flexibility, but not necessary.
Tapestry needle

**GAUGE**
16 sts and 24 rows = 4" in St st
14 sts and 32 rows = 4" in Garter st
Always check and MATCH gauge for best fit.

### SECTION 3

With RS facing, using A, pick up and knit 5 sts along edge of 2A Triangle and 5 sts along edge of 2B Triangle—10 sts; beg Garter st.

Row 1 and all WS rows: Knit.

Rows 2, 4 and 6: Ssk, knit across to last 2 sts, k2tog.

Row 8: Ssk, k2tog.

Row 10: K2tog.

Row 12: Pull loop through rem st to secure.

Using rem 3 CC, work as above, using B along edges of 2B and 2C; C along edges of 2C and 2D; D along edges of 2D and 2A.

### SECTION 4

With RS facing, using A, pick up and knit 7 sts along edge of A Triangle and 7 sts along edge of B Triangle from previous section—14 sts; beg Garter st.

Row 1 and all WS rows: Knit.

Row 2: Work as Section 3, Row 2.

Cont in Garter st, dec 1 st at each side EOR as for Section 3; end last row as for Row 12—no sts rem.

Using rem 3 CC, work as above, using B along edges of B and C; C along edges of C and D; D along edges of D and A from previous section.

### SECTION 5

With RS facing, pick up and knit 9 sts along edges of Triangles from previous section—18 sts; work as for Section 4.

### SECTION 6

With RS facing, pick up and knit 11 sts along edges of Triangles from previous section—22 sts; work as for Section 4.

### SECTION 7

With RS facing, pick up and knit 13 sts along edges of Triangles from previous section—26 sts; beg as for Section 4, then complete each piece as foll:

**Lower edge (7A):** When piece measures 1 (2, 3)" from pick up row; bind off all sts loosely.

**Left side edge (7B) and Right side edge (7D):** When piece measures 1 (1½, 2)" from pick up row; bind off all sts loosely.

**Front Neck edge (7C):** When piece measures 1" from pick up row, end with a RS row—18 sts; pm each side of center 6 sts.

**Shape Neck:** (WS) Work across to marker; join a second ball of yarn and bind off center 6 sts for neck; work to end. Working both sides at same time, with separate balls of yarn, cont on 6 rem sts on each side as foll:

Row 1: (RS) Ssk, k2, k2tog.

Row 2 and all WS rows: Knit.

Row 3: Ssk, k2tog.

Row 5: K2tog.

Row 7: Pull loop through rem st to secure.

### SECTION 8

**Corners:** With RS facing, using color indicated, pick up and knit sts as foll for each piece; work as for Section 4.

**Lower LH corner (8A):** Using A, pick up and knit 6 (10, 14) sts along edge of 7A; pick up and knit 6 (8, 10) sts along edge of 7B—12 (18, 24) sts.

FRONT
DIAGRAM

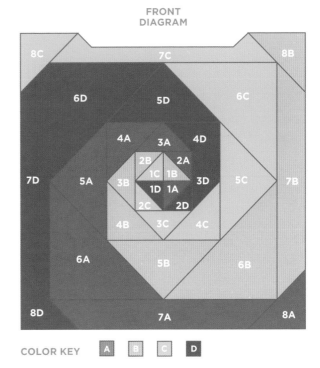

COLOR KEY    A  B  C  D

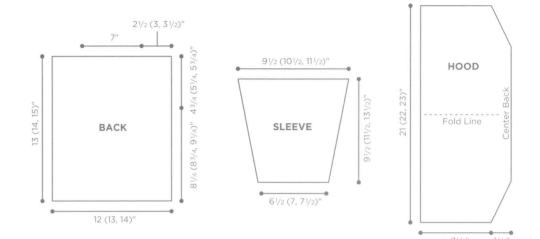

**Lower RH Corner (8D):** Using D, pick up and knit 6 (8, 10) sts along edge of 7D; pick up and knit 6 (10, 14) sts along edge of 7A—12 (18, 24) sts.

**Left Shoulder (8B):** Using B, pick up and knit 6 (8, 10) sts along edge of 7B; pick up and knit 14 sts along edge of 7C—20 (22, 24) sts.

**Right Shoulder (8C):** Using C, pick up and knit 14 sts along edge of 7C; pick up and knit 6 (8, 10) sts along edge of 7D—20 (22, 24) sts.

**Lower Front Edge:** Using MC, pick up and knit 48 (52, 56) sts along lower edge; work in Garter st for 1". Bind off.

### BACK
Using MC, cast on 48 (52, 56) sts; beg Garter st. Work even for 1". Change to St st; work even until piece measures 14" from beg. Bind off all sts loosely.

### SLEEVES
Using MC, cast on 26 (28, 30) sts; beg Garter st. Work even for 1". Change to St st.

**Shape Sleeve:** Inc 1 st each side every 4th row 6 (7, 8) times—38 (42, 46) sts.

Work even until piece measures 9½ (11½, 13½)" from beg, or desired length; bind off all sts loosely.

### HOOD
Using MC, cast on 30 sts; beg St st.

**Shape Hood:** (RS) Inc 1 st at beg RS rows (center back of Hood) every 4th row 6 times—36 sts.

Work even until piece measures 17 (18, 19)" from beg, end with a WS row.

(RS) Dec 1 st at beg RS rows every 4th row 6 times—30 sts.

Work even until piece measures 21 (22, 23)" from beg. Bind off all sts loosely.

### FINISHING
Block pieces with steam—Front may appear a bit concave, but will flatten out. Sew shoulder seams (2½ [3, 3½]" from each armhole edge), leave rem 7" open for neck. Measure down from shoulder seam, Front and Back, 4¾ (5½, 5¾)", pm; sew sleeves between markers. Sew side and sleeve seams.

Fold Hood in half on fold line, matching shaping; sew center Back seam. Fit hood around neck, folding Front edge to WS for about 1" on each side. Sew Hood in place.

# paisley carpetbag

## OVERVIEW

To make this bag, Paisleys are knit individually from the center out, and are composed of 4 layers of different colors—for speed you may want to knit several centers, then work Layer 1 around each, then Layer 2 around each, then Border around each—or you may want to knit one at a time. On Layer 2, the piece is joined to knit in rnds. When you cut yarn, leave about 2" for sewing seam at Paisley's crook. Do not knit too tightly, and give plenty of slack to yo's; otherwise it will be hard to ease needle into sts around curves, as the yarn has little elasticity.

## COLORWAYS

Colors listed in following order: Center Teardrop/Layer 1/Layer2/Border.

Colorway 1: F/A/D/G; Colorway 2: B/D/E/A; Colorway 3: G/F/C/B; Colorway 4: D/C/G/F; Colorway 5: E/B/A/C; Colorway 6: C/B/A/E; Odd colorways: C/G/B/E; C/B/G/E; C/F/B/E; C/B/F/E

Make 54 pieces—choose your favorites, or to arrange as shown on diagram, make 10 pieces in Colorway 1; 9 pieces in Colorways 2, 3, 4, and 5; 4 pieces in Colorway 6; 1 piece in each of the odd Colorways.

## SIZE
One Size

### KNITTED MEASUREMENTS

Bag is 22" wide at base and 12" tall to handle (each bag will vary depending on angle of paisleys).

Each paisley is 4" wide at widest point from tip to curve and 3½" tall at tallest part of the curve.

## YARN
Rowan "Summer Tweed" (70% silk/30% cotton), 2-ply worsted

1 hank each (1.75oz/50g; 118yd/108m) in 514 reed (ochre) (A); 504 gold (yellow) (B); 523 legend (dk. olive) (C); 522 smoulder (wine) (D); 528 brilliant (fuchsia) (E); 509 sunset (coral) (F); 526 angel (pink) (G)

## NEEDLES/TOOLS
One set of five US 6 (4mm) double-pointed needles* [dpn], or size to match gauge

*or 2 circular needles

Tapestry needle or crochet hook for weaving ends

## NOTIONS
Sewing needle and silk thread in color to match A or F for sewing paisleys and lining
*Optional: Sewing machine makes lining faster.*

1½ yd silk brocade fabric

2 wooden handles, 12" wide with 10" slat—style #32175, M&J Trimming (see Resources)

Iron (to press lining)

## GAUGE
18 sts and 24 rows = 4" in St st

Always check and MATCH gauge for best results.

## PAISLEY

### CENTER TEARDROP

Using long-tail cast-on method and proper color, cast on 4 sts.

**Row 1:** (RS) K4; using single cast-on method, cast on 3 sts at end of row —7 sts.

**Row 2:** Knit.

**Row 3:** Knit.

**Row 4:** Bind off 4 sts; sl st on RH needle used for bind off to LH needle, k3tog-tbl—1 st rem on RH needle.

Pick up and knit 1 st in side edge of Row 2, pick up and knit 1 st inside edge of cast on row; insert LH needle from back to front through the 3 sts on RH needle and k3tog-tbl.

Pick up and knit 1 st in nearest st of cast on row, pick up and knit 1 st in next st of cast on row; insert LH needle from back to front through the 3 sts on RH needle and k3tog-tbl.

Pick up and knit 1 st in 3rd st of cast on row, pick up and knit 1 st in 4th st of cast on row; insert LH needle from back to front through the 3 sts on RH needle and k3tog-tbl. Cut yarn; run tail through last st to secure, then run through st on cast on row.

### PAISLEY

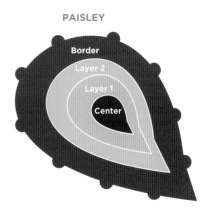

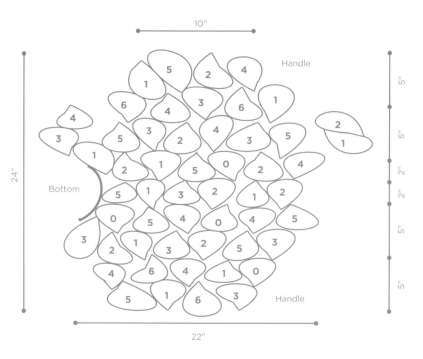

### LAYER 1

Turn Center Teardrop to RS—with the last st pointing up, the tip points to the right and curve points to the left.

Using dpn (or 2 circular needles) and proper color, beg in crook of curve where last piece ended, work around edge counterclockwise, picking up and knitting sts in the back loops of the edge sts as foll:

(RS) [K1, yo, k1, yo, k1] in each of the next 5 edge sts; [k1, yo, k1] in each of the next 4 sts;—now you are at the tip—[k1, yo, k1] in each of the next 2 sts—you are at the beg of the rnd, turn to WS.

(WS) Bind off 2 sts (these sts will be sewn into the crook of the curve), then knit each st around, working each yo as a st—41 sts. Cut yarn.

### LAYER 2

Turn piece to RS. Using proper color, purl; this will create a decorative effect, as the color at the bottom of the st peeps below the top of the last layer; at the end of the row you will be at the crook.

Instead of turning for a WS row, beg to work in rnds.

Pm for beg of rnd; join by knitting into the st on needle to left, which was first st of row, with the yarn on right, extending from st just worked; k21, wrap next st, turn.

(WS) K21, turn.

(RS) Knit to end of rnd. This Short Row shaping emphasizes the curve. Cut yarn.

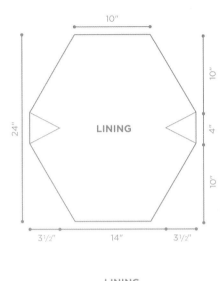

LINING

10"
24"
10"
4"
10"
3½"    14"    3½"

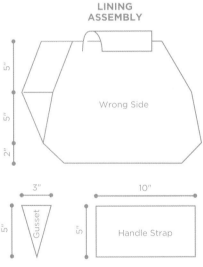

LINING ASSEMBLY

5"
5"
2"

Wrong Side

3"    10"

5"    5"

Gusset    Handle Strap

### BORDER

Cont in rnds, using proper color, k36—you are at Paisley tip—[k1, yo, k1] in next 3 sts, k to end.

Next Rnd: Bind off 1; * make a bobble by: ([k1, yo, k1, yo, k1] into next st, insert LH needle from back to front through 2 nearest loops on RH needle, k2tog-tbl—4 loops rem;

insert LH needle from back to front through 2 nearest loops on RH needle, k2tog-tbl—3 loops rem; insert LH needle from back to front through 3 nearest loops on RH needle, k3tog-tbl); bind off 4 sts, beg with the st before the bobble by: (pass that st over st from bobble; knit next st, pass bobble st over new st; knit next st, pass previous st over this st; knit next st, pass previous st over this st); rep from * until 8 bobbles have been worked—you are at the tip, where on last rnd, each of the next 3 sts was increased to 3 sts; discontinue the bobble sequence, but cont to bind off, working the 3 sts as foll: K2tog, bind off; k1, bind off—there are 5 more sts to rnd; bind off 1, (4th st from end must be knit for this), then make a bobble in the 3rd st from end; bind off rem sts—1 loop rem; make a bobble into first st of rnd below (first rnd in this color); bind off. Cut yarn and run through to secure—total of 10 bobbles.

### FINISHING

Sew inner seam of each Paisley by running through ends of proper color.

Arrange Paisleys as shown, trying to vary direction each Paisley points and fit to dimensions shown. Sew edges with sewing needle and thread. Do not sew together the last round of border, but keep as much paisley surrounding seam as possible; work Mattress st from RS, or Whip st from WS, through the perimeter of bind off. Before adding side pieces, place piece flat along the grain of the lining fabric and outline with a ⁵⁄₈" seam allowance; do not indent at bottom, but draw a straight line from the widest point—the extra fabric will be folded in to help form the gusset.

### LINING

Cut out lining piece, plus 2 gusset pieces and 2 handle strap pieces, adding seam allowance to given measurements. Keep in mind that the RS of lining fabric will show inside the bag; the WS will face the WS of Paisleys, and the raw ends of the handle straps and other seams will be hidden between the Paisleys and the lining.

Handles: Stitch the handle strap, with WS facing and with the seam allowances pressed to the WS, to the WS of lining at center top (RS of strap faces WS of lining, so both RS's are facing away). Insert strap through handle from back to front, and fold to front. Stitch close to the bottom of the handle and trim seam. Repeat for other handle.

At center of lining piece, bottom of bag, fold sides in as shown to form corner. With RS's tog, stitch from WS. Insert gusset pieces at sides, and sew to lining, leaving approx 5" open to handle. Press all seam allowances to WS.

Fit lining inside Paisley bag and, with sewing needle and thread, whip st along all edges, hiding most of the handle straps and gussets with Paisleys.

# zip-off color-block yoke sweater

## OVERVIEW

The Sweater is knit in segments, from hem to armhole; sleeves are knit in segments to armhole, then the yoke is knit to the neck like an Icelandic yoke sweater—except you're not actually working in-the-round, but working in rows with a separate ball of yarn for each color segment. On the Body segments, for every decrease at the edge of one color block there is a matching increase on other, so that they will fit together when a zipper is sewn in on the diagonal to connect them. There is a severe rate of decrease and increase—2 sts each side every row—but this tubular yarn allows for double decreases and increases without bulk; it collapses in and is very flexible. Be careful to give the increases, decreases, and edge stitches enough yarn so that the edges do not pull in lengthwise. Make sure that the cast on and bind off edges do not pull in, as the zippers will be sewn along these as well.

## PIECE 1—LOWER BODY

Using A, cast on 140 sts. Pm on RH needle for beg of round; slip marker (sl m) every rnd. Join, being careful not to twist sts. Beg St st; Work even until piece measures 2" from beg.

**Next Rnd:** Bind off 2 sts, work to end—138 sts; remove marker, turn. Beg working in rows.

**Shape Diagonal Edge:** Cont in St st, dec 2 sts each side every row as foll:

**Row 1:** (WS) P1 (selvedge st), p3tog, p to last 4 sts, p3tog-tbl, p1 (selvedge st)—134 sts.

**Row 2:** K1, k3tog-tbl, k to last 4 sts, k3tog, k1—130 sts.

| SIZE | YARN | NEEDLES/TOOLS | NOTIONS | GAUGE |
|---|---|---|---|---|
| One Size, Unisex | Needful Yarns/King "Modigliani" (100% merino), bulky tubular chainette | US 10½ (6.5mm) 32" long circular, or size to match gauge | Six size 5 separating zippers with black tape, silver teeth, and ¾" zipper pull ring in the following lengths: Two 40" long, two 13" long, two 14" long (see Resources) | 14 sts and 16 rnds/rows = 4" in St st |
| **KNITTED MEASUREMENTS** | 6 balls (1.75oz/50g; 71yd/65m) each in 09 black/white marled (A) and 19 black/gray print (B); | US 10½ (6.5mm) 12" long circular (or use 2 longer circulars alternating as with dpn) for sleeves | | Always check and MATCH gauge for best fit. |
| Chest: 40" | 4 balls in 03 beige heather (C) | Stitch markers | Straight pins | |
| Length: 25" | | Stitch holders/spare circular needles | Sewing needle and strong thread to match A, B and C; bright color thread for basting | |
| Sleeve at upper arm: 13" | | Crochet hook size J/10 (6mm) | | |

Rep Rows 1 and 2 until a total of 34 dec rows have been worked—2 sts rem. *Note: On final dec row, forgo the selvedge sts.*

Bind off rem sts—piece should measure 10½" at longer side.

## PIECE 2
Using B, cast on 2 sts. Beg St st; inc 2 st each side every row as foll:

**Row 1:** (WS) Purl into front, back, and front of each st—6 sts.

**Row 2:** K1 (selvedge st), knit into front, back, and front of next st (inc 2), k2, inc 2 in next st, k1 (selvedge st)—10 sts.

**Row 3:** P1, purl into front, back, and front of next st (inc 2), purl to last 2 sts, inc 2 in next st, p1—14 sts.

**Row 4:** K1, inc 2 in next st, knit to last 2 sts, inc 2 in next st, k1—18 sts.

Rep Rows 3 and 4 until a total of 34 inc rows have been worked—138 sts; piece should measure 8½" at longer side, and AT SAME TIME, on last (RS) row, cast on 2 sts at end of row—140 sts; pm for beg of rnd, join. Beg working in rnds.

Work even in St st for 4½"; bind off all sts loosely.

## SLEEVES
### PIECE 3—LOWER LEFT SLEEVE
Using B, cast on 46 sts. Pm on RH needle for beg of round; sl m every

rnd. Join, being careful not to twist sts. Beg St st; work even until piece measures 14½" from beg. Bind off all sts loosely. *Sleeves are oversized—and extend over the hands. If desired, shorten Pieces 3 and 4 by 2" or 3" each.*

## PIECE 4—LOWER RIGHT SLEEVE
Using C, cast on and work as for Piece 3 until piece measures 8" from beg. Bind off all sts loosely.

## PIECE 5—UPPER LEFT SLEEVE
Using C, cast on and work as for Piece 3 until piece measures 4½" from beg.

**Next Rnd:** Bind off 13 sts, work to end; remove marker, cast on 28 sts at end of row for Front Yoke—61 sts, turn. Beg working in rows.

**Next Row:** (WS) Purl to end; cast on 29 sts at end of row for Back Yoke—90 sts.

Work even for 4 rows in St st, end with a WS row. Place sts on spare needle, do not cut yarn.

## PIECE 6—UPPER RIGHT SLEEVE
Using A, cast on and work as for Piece 3 until piece measures 11" from beg.

**Next Rnd:** Bind off 13 sts, work to end; remove marker, cast on 28 sts at end of row for Back Yoke—61 sts, turn. Beg working in rows.

**Next Row:** (WS) Purl to end; cast on 29 sts at end of row for Front Yoke—90 sts.

Work even for 4 rows in St st, end with a WS row.

## YOKE
**Row 1:** (RS) Decrease Row—Cont in St st, with RS of Piece 6 facing, using A, [k13, k2tog] 6 times—84 sts; with RS facing, take up Piece 5, and using C, work as for Piece 6—84 sts.

**Rows 2-4:** Work even as est.

**Row 5:** Decrease Row—Cont in St st with colors as est, on each piece, [k12, k2tog] 6 times—78 sts each piece.

Rep Rows 2-5, dec 6 sts on each piece every 4th row, 7 more times—36 sts rem each piece.

## NECK
Work even for 4½" more; bind off rem sts loosely.

## FINISHING
Block lightly with steam.

Work 1 row single crochet along edges of pieces.

Pin, baste, and sew in zippers as foll:

**Lower Body:** Place one 40" long zipper on a diagonal between pieces 1 and 2, beg lower right Front with the zipper pull, cont up to left Front, around to Back, and down to lower right Back.

**Sleeves:** With the zipper pull at center outside of Sleeve, place one 13" long zipper around right Sleeve, between Pieces 4 and 6; one around left Sleeve, between Pieces 3 and 5.

**Yoke:** With the zipper pull at upper edge of neck, place one 14" long "zipper on Front between pieces 5 and 6; the other on Back between pieces 5 and 6. (When sewing zipper around chest, layer it over the bodice zipper to hide the bodice zipper— back bodice will not open.)

**Chest:** Place rem 40" long zipper, beg at left center Front, with zipper pull at right center Front, horizontally around chest, between Pieces 2, 5, and 6, leaving underarm bind off sts open.

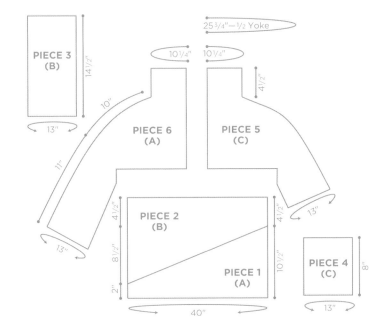

# slip-stitch intarsia kilt

## OVERVIEW

Kilt is worked from waist to hem in one piece. RS rows begin at the inner left Front placket, work around left hip, to Back, then to right hip and end at the outer right Front placket. Paired increases are worked at each hip; all incs are in MC areas. New sts should be worked in pattern.

## SPECIAL TECHNIQUE
**Slipstitch Intarsia Check/Plaid**

While working in Slip Stitch patt, you create vertical stripes in a check pattern, using separate small balls of each CC, which are used for 2 rows of the 4-row Stitch pattern rep. The MC is not stranded behind these areas; use separate balls of MC as well. When Rows 3 and 4 are worked using MC only, use the first ball of MC, which will be returned to its place after the WS row. Horizontal stripes and crossed areas are created by introducing a new ball of one CC on Rows 3 and 4 over all sts. Then Rows 1 and 2 are worked using separate balls of MC and CC(s).

**SIZES**

Small (Medium, Large)
**Shown in Medium.**

**KNITTED MEASUREMENTS**
**Low waist/high hip:** 27 ¾ (30, 34½)" (closed—there is 5" overlap, so buckles can be adjusted)
**Low Hip:** 35 ¾ (38, 42½)"
**Hem:** 41¾ (44, 48½)"
**Length:** 15"

**YARN**

Crystal Palace "Iceland" (100% wool), bulky singles

3 (4, 4) balls (3.5oz/ 100g; 109yd/100m) in 8166 sienna (A) as MC

2 balls in 9719 claret (B) as CC

1 ball each in 6320 leaf (C) and 1015 white (D) as CCs

**NEEDLES/TOOLS**

US 11 (8mm) 32" long circular, or size to match gauge

Stitch markers

**NOTIONS**

2 metal buckles

Flat trouser-band type hook and eye for waist-band closure

Sewing needle or sewing machine and thread to match A

**GAUGE**

14 sts and 28 rows = 4" in Slip Stitch patt

*Note: When measuring gauge, count each triangular check as 2 rows (slip 1 row, then knit 1 row); the 4-row rep of pattern creates 2 staggered rows of triangles.*

Always check and MATCH gauge for best fit.

## STITCH PATTERN

**Slip Stitch Pattern** (over even number sts)

**Row 1:** (RS) Establishing MC and CC per instructions, * wyib, k1, wyif, slip 1; rep from * to end—be sure to bring the new color over the previous color, so there aren't holes between colors.

**Row 2:** Cont colors as est, * wyif, p1, wyib, slip 1; rep from * to end.

**Row 3:** Using color indicated in instructions, * wyib, k1, wyif, slip 1; rep from * to end.

**Row 4:** With the same color as Row 3, *wyif, p1, wyib, slip 1; rep from * to end.

*Note: In areas where a vertical and horizontal stripe of the same color meet, the intersection is solids, all other areas should appear perfectly checked. As each area has even number of sts, you will always beg with a knit st and end with a slip st for each color, making it easy to tell if you are off pattern.*

Rep Rows 1–4 for Slip st patt.

**Preparation:** Wind off 8 small reels of A, 3 small reels of B and D, and 2 small reels of C.

Using long-tail cast-on method and a full ball A, cast on 114 (122, 138) sts for waist.

**Preparation Row:** (WS) Cont with A, * wyif, p1, wyib, slip 1; rep from * to end. Beg Slip st patt.

**Row 1:** (RS) With A, work 14 (16, 20) sts; with D, work 4 sts; with a new reel of A, work 4 sts; with B, work 6 sts; with a new reel of A, work 2 sts, place marker (pm) for left hip, with same reel of A, work 4 sts; with D, work 2 sts; with a new reel of A, work 6 (8, 12) sts; with C, work 4 sts; with a new reel of A, work 8 (10, 14) sts; with B, work 8 sts; with a new reel of A, work 16 sts, pm for right hip, with same reel of A, work 6 sts; with C, work 4 sts; with a new reel of A, work 6 sts; with B, work 8 sts; with a new reel of A, work 4 sts; with D, work 2 sts; with a new reel of A, work 6 (8, 12) sts.

**Row 2 and all WS rows:** Work even as est.

**Row 3:** Increase Row—With A, *work across to 1 st before maker, inc (knit into front and back of next st [k-f/b]), slip marker (sl m), inc; rep from * once, work to end—4 sts increased; 118 (126, 142) sts.

**Row 5:** Est colors as Row 1, working inc sts in A and slipping markers.

**Row 7:** With B, work all sts.

**Row 9:** Est colors as Row 1, working inc sts in A and slipping markers.

**Row 11:** Increase Row—With B, work as Row 3—122 (130, 146) sts.

**Row 13:** Est colors as Row 1, working inc sts in A and slipping markers.

**Row 15:** With B, work all sts.

**Row 16:** Rep Row 2.

Cont shaping as est, inc 1 st each side of markers every 8th row 6 times more, for a total of 8 Increase Rows—146 (154, 170) sts and AT SAME TIME, work the foll Color Sequence on Rows 3 and 4, cont Rows 1 and 2 as est:

Use A for 5 reps of Rows 3 and 4; D for 1 rep; A for 3 reps; B for 3 reps; A for 2 reps; C for 2 reps; A for 3 reps; D for 1 rep; then cont with A until piece measures 15" from beg (should be 1 rep more). Do not bind off.

## FINISHING

**Loopy Fringe Hem:** Slip sts off needle; with thread to match A, hand or machine stitch through the edge of the row previous to the open sts. Try on Kilt and overlap right Front over left Front; place the buckles along the opening where they can be comfortably adjusted. Sew hook and eye to top waistband.

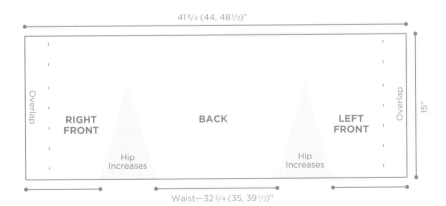

# large-scale herringbone pullover

**SIZES**
Small (Medium, Large)
**Shown in Small.**

**KNITTED
MEASUREMENTS**
**Chest/Waist:** 36 (40, 44)"
**Length:** 23 (23½, 23½)"
**Sleeve at upper arm:** 13¼
(14½, 16)"

**YARN**
Plymouth/Indiecita "Alpaca
Bouclé" (90% alpaca/10%
nylon), bulky bouclé
6 (7, 7) balls (1.75oz/50g;
70yd/64m) in 13 brown/
gray (A)
2 (2, 3) balls each in
12 tan/brown (B), 19
pink/magenta (C), 18
magenta/orange (D)

**NEEDLES/TOOLS**
US 10 (6mm) needles, or
size to match gauge
US 10 (6mm) 16" long
circular
Stitch markers
Tapestry needle

**GAUGE**
12 sts and 22 rows = 4" in
St st
Always check and MATCH
gauge for best fit.

**STITCH PATTERN**
**Herringbone:** see Chart

**BACK**
Using A, cast on 54 (60, 66) sts.
Beg 2x2 Rib; work even until piece
measures 1½" from beg, end with a
WS row.

**Establish pattern:** (RS) Beg Herringbone Chart, Row 1, in St st; work
18 (20, 22)-st rep 3 times across,
working each color section with a
separate strand of yarn, intarsia
method; wrap new color around
previous color to prevent holes.

Cont as est, work Rows 2–64 of
Chart, then work 64-row rep for rem
of piece, and AT SAME TIME, when
piece measures 14½ (14½, 14)" from
beg, end with a WS row.

**Shape Armholes:** (RS) Bind off 2 (3,
4) sts beg of next 2 rows, then dec 1
st each side EOR 4 (5, 6) times—42
(44, 46) sts. Work even until armhole
measures 7½ (8, 8½)" from beg of
shaping, end with a WS row.

**Shape Shoulders and Neck:** Bind off
4 sts beg next 2 rows, 3 sts beg of
next 4 rows—22 (24, 26) sts rem for
neck; bind off neck sts.

**FRONT**
Work as for Back until piece measures
20½ (21, 21)"—42 (44, 46) sts, end
with a WS row; pm each side of
center 8 (10, 12) sts.

**Shape Neck and Shoulders:** Cont as
est from Chart, work across to
marker; join a second ball of yarn,
bind off center sts for neck; work to
end; pm at center Front neck edge
for Collar. Working both sides at
same time, with separate balls of
yarn, at each neck edge, dec 1 st
every row 4 times, then EOR 3 times,

and AT SAME TIME, when armhole measures same as Back to shoulder shaping, end with a WS row.

**Shape Shoulders:** as for Back, while completing neck shaping.

### SLEEVES

Using A, cast on 26 (28, 28) sts; beg 2x2 Rib. Work even for 7 rows, end with a WS row.

**Shape Sleeve:** Inc 1 st each side this row, then every 8th row 7 (8, 10) times total—40 (44, 48) sts.

Work even until piece measures 18″ from beg, end with a WS row.

**Shape Sleeve Cap:** Bind off 2 (3, 4) sts beg next 2 rows, then dec 1 st each side EOR 4 (5, 6) times.

Work even for 1 (1½, 2)″, end with a WS row.

Dec 1 st each side EOR 8 (7, 6) times—12 (14, 16) sts. Bind off rem sts.

### FINISHING

Graft shoulder seams. Sew side and sleeve seams. Set in sleeves. Weave in ends.

### COLLAR

With RS facing, using circular needle and A, beg 3 sts to the right of the marker at center Front neck, working from right to left toward center Front, pick up and knit 44 (48, 52) sts around neck to beg of pick up; cast on 6 sts with simple cast on—50 (54, 58) sts. Beg St st.

**Row 1:** (WS) Purl.

**Row 2:** K1, ssk, k to last 3 sts, k2tog, k1.

**Row 3:** P1, p2tog, p to last 3 sts, p2tog, p1. Bind off all sts loosely, knitwise.

Overlap the cast on sts behind the Collar edge, 3 sts each side of center Front marker; stitch neatly in place on WS.

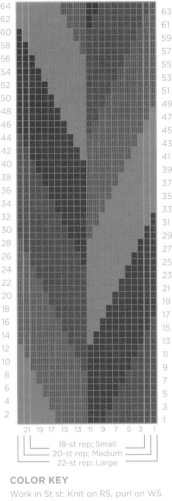

**HERRINGBONE CHART**

18-st rep; Small
20-st rep; Medium
22-st rep; Large

**COLOR KEY**

Work in St st: Knit on RS, purl on WS.

A: brown/gray
B: tan/brown
C: pink/magenta
D: magenta/orange

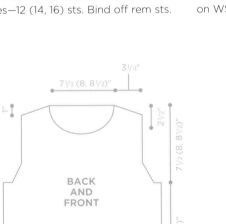

BACK AND FRONT

SLEEVE

# reversible double-knit vest

## OVERVIEW

Vest is worked in 3 pieces, 2 Fronts and Back, in Double-knit, creating 2 fabric faces of St st, making the vest reversible. A circular needle is used, although piece is worked in rows, to facilitate sliding the stitches to the opposite end of the needle in order to work the second color Side of each row. A cable needle is employed, where necessary, to rearrange the sts, so that 2 sts of the same color can be worked together for shaping; the bound off/cast on holes are also worked with the help of a cable needle.

## GAUGE SWATCH

Although both faces of the Double-knit fabric are worked in St st, gauge cannot be measured accurately by working a St st swatch with one color.

Using both colors, cast on 16 sts with each color (see instructions for Back). Work in Double-knit as given for Back until swatch measures 4½" from the beg. BO all sts. Measure gauge on both faces to be sure you are working with an even tension.

## SPECIAL TECHNIQUES

**Double-knit** (see Chart on page 168)

All rows are worked twice, once with color A, once with color B, making the resulting fabric reversible. In order to clarify the instructions, one Side (the Side with B hem and A body) has been designated as the RS of the piece. The Chart shows sts as they appear on the Side (color A or B) that is facing. Read all rows shown on the Chart from right to left; stitch numbers represent each pair of stitches—one A st and one B st per pair. *VERY IMPORTANT: When slipping stitches, the yarn should remain*

## SIZES

Small, Medium, Large
**Shown in Small.**

## KNITTED MEASUREMENTS

Chest/Waist: 37 (41, 45)"
Length: 22 (22½, 23)"

## YARN

Heirloom "Easy Care 8-ply" (100% merino), worsted

5 (7, 9) balls (1.75oz/50g; 106yd/98m) in 794 garnet (A)

Heirloom "Aristocrat 8-ply" (50% mohair/50% wool), worsted

3 (4, 5) balls (1.75oz/50g; 124yd/115m) in 324 poppy (B)

## NEEDLES/TOOLS

Size US 8 (5mm) 24–36" long circular needle, or size to match gauge

Cable needle (cn)

Tapestry needle

## GAUGE

15 sts and 20 rows = 4" in Double-knit St st

Always check and MATCH gauge for best fit.

*between the 2 Sides of the fabric; DO NOT wrap colors around each other, except at the beg of each new row.*

Work each row from Chart as foll:

Using the facing color, knit the MC (facing color) sts and slip the CC (non-facing color) sts as foll:

Balls of both colors are at the RH end of needle, ready to work from Chart, reading from right to left; the first st is MC—Wrap yarns to join side; using MC as working yarn, * k1-MC, slip 1-CC wyif; rep from * to end of row. Slide sts to RH end of needle.

Using non-facing color, slip the MC sts wyib and purl CC sts as foll:

Ball of MC is now at LH end of needle, CC is at RH end, ready to work from Chart, reading from right to left; first st is MC—Using CC as working yarn, * sl 1-MC wyib, p1-CC; rep from * to end of row, turn.

Cont in this manner, working each row of Chart twice, once with each color.

### BACK

Using long-tail cast-on method, and one strand each of A and B, cast on 68 (76, 84) sts alternately with each color, beg color A—136 (152, 168) sts.

### CONTRAST COLOR HEM

Turn cast on edge so both balls of yarn are at RH end of needle; first st is color B.

**Establish Pattern:** (RS) B-Side facing; beg Double-knit from Chart, Row 1 (see Special Techniques at left)—Using B as working yarn (MC), work 2 (0, 2) pairs of sts in Double-knit, work 16-st rep of Chart 4 (4, 5) times, work 2 (12, 2) pairs of sts in Double-knit. Complete Row 1, then work Row 2 from Chart.

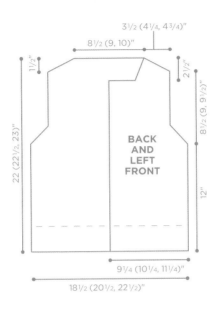

BACK AND LEFT FRONT

3½ (4¼, 4¾)"

8½ (9, 10)"

1½"

2½"

8½ (9, 9½)"

12"

22 (22½, 23)"

9¼ (10¼, 11¼)"

18½ (20½, 22½)"

**Establish Hole Pattern**, Row 3: (RS) B-Side facing—Using B, cont as est, ** work across Chart to St 12, beg of Hole; work Bind Off for Holes as foll: Knit st 12 with B, then slip B-st to cn, hold to front; slip 1 A-st wyif; k1 B-st and slip to cn, then pass 1st st on cn over 2nd to bind off 1 st; leave rem st on cn at front of work, * slip 1 A-st wyif; k1 B-st and slip to cn, bind off as before; rep from * twice more—4 sts bound off; slip B-st rem on cn to RH needle (the A-sts which were slipped are side-by-side, with no B-sts between). Rep from ** 3 (3, 4) times, work in Double-knit to end. Slide sts to RH end of needle.

Row 3, B-Side still facing: Using A, work even as est—slip all B-sts wyib and purl all A-sts, turn.

Row 4: (WS) A-Side facing—Using A, work as for first part of Row 3, working holes beg at St 12 of each 16-st rep of Chart. Slide sts to RH end of needle.

Row 4, A-Side still facing: Using B, work as est, and AT SAME TIME, cast

on 4 sts over bound off sts for Holes as foll: * Slip 1 A-st wyib; cast on 1 B-st using single cast-on method, by looping yarn over thumb and placing loop on RH needle; rep from * 3 times—4 sts cast on; slip 1 A-st wyib, work to end, turn.

Row 5: (RS) B-Side facing—Using B, work even as est. Slide sts to RH end of needle.

Row 5, B-Side still facing: Using A, work as est, and AT SAME TIME, cast on 4 sts over bound off sts for Holes as foll: * Slip 1 B-st wyib; cast on 1 A-st; rep from * 3 times—4 sts cast on; slip 1 B-st wyib.

Cont as est from Chart, working 1-st and 3-st Holes as given for 4-st Hole, with appropriate number of sts. Work until piece measures 3" from beg, end with a RS row.

### Reverse Colors for Body

(WS) With A-Side facing, using B, k2tog across—68 (76, 84) B-sts. Slide sts to RH end of needle.

Using A, * slip 1 B-st wyib; pick up and purl 1 A-st as foll: Wyif, insert RH needle into nearest loop of the A-st from the row below (which is under the B-st in the k2tog pair), and purl; rep from *, forming the last A-st by working into the outer edge of the A-st from the row below—68 (76, 84) sts each color. The first st at RH side of row is B; this is a WS row with B-Side facing, turn.

(RS) A-Side is facing; cont as est from Chart, work through Row 30, then rep Rows 1–30 for rem of piece; and AT SAME TIME, when piece measures 12" from beg, end with a WS row.

**Shape Armholes:** (RS) Wrap yarns to join sides; using A, [k1, sl 1 wyif] twice; work ssk on next 2 A-sts as foll: slip next A-st knitwise to RH needle, slip next B-st to cn, hold to back, slip next A-st knitwise to RH needle, insert LH needle into the front of the 2 sts on RH needle and k2tog-tbl; sl B-st from cn to RH needle; cont as est in Double-knit to last 4 pairs of sts rem; work k2tog on next 2 A-sts as foll: slip next A-st purlwise to RH needle, slip next B-st to cn, hold to back, return A-st to LH needle, k2tog; slip st from cn to RH needle, work as est to end. Slide sts to RH end of needle.

Using B, [sl 1 wyib, p1] twice; slip A-st (from the decrease) wyib; work p2tog on next 2 B-sts; work as est to last 6 sts (2 B-sts side-by-side), p2tog-tbl, work to end.

Cont to dec at each edge on both color Sides in this manner every RS row 4 more times—58 (66, 74) sts each color rem. Work even until arm-hole measures 8½ (9, 9½)" from beg of shaping, end with a WS row.

**Shape Shoulders:** Beg RS row, bind off 13 (16, 18) sts from each shoulder over the next 8 rows as foll: At arm-hole edge, bind off 4 (5, 6) sts once, 4 (4, 5) sts once, 3 (4, 4) sts once, then 2 (3, 3) sts once, working as for Bind Off for Holes.

### LEFT FRONT
### CONTRAST COLOR HEM

Working as for Back, cast on 34 (38, 42) sts with each color—68 (76, 84) sts. Beg Double-knit.

**Establish Pattern:** (RS) Work 1 (3, 0) pairs of sts, work 2 (2, 2) 16-st rep from Chart, end 0 (3, 10) pairs of sts. Cont as est, work even until piece measures 3" from beg, end with a WS row.

Reverse Colors for Body as for Back.

Cont as est until piece measures 12" from beg, end with a WS row.

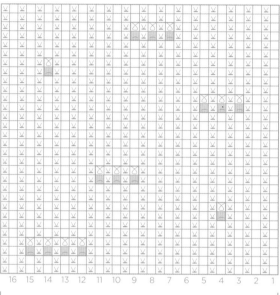

Repeat of 16 pairs of stitches

**KEY**

Work all rows from right to left, (see Special Technique).

Each row is worked twice, once with each color. Symbols indicate first; then second time worked.

☐ Knit 1 with facing color; slip 1 purlwise wyib.

☑ Slip 1 purlwise wyif; p1 with non-facing color.

▦ Bind off 1 st.

⊠ Cast on 1 st over bound off st, using color of bound off st.

**Shape Armhole:** (RS) At armhole edge, dec 1 st EOR 5 times as for Back.

Work even until armhole measures 7½ (8, 8½)" from beg of shaping, end with a RS row.

**Shape Neck:** (WS) Bind off 12 (13, 15) sts from each facing Side as for Bind Off for Holes.

Keeping the 2 Sides connected, at neck edge, dec 1 st EOR 4 times, working as for armhole decs; and AT SAME TIME, when armhole measures 8½ (9, 9½)" from beg of shaping, end with a WS row.

**Shape Shoulder:** as for Back.

### RIGHT FRONT

Work as for left Front, reversing all shaping; beg Row 21 of Chart, so that the Hole placement is more varied.

### COLLAR

Cast on 58 (62, 66) sts each A and B, alternating as for Back—116 (124, 132) sts. Work in Double-knit until Collar measures 1¾" from beg, end with B-Side facing. With A-Side facing, using B, k2tog across row—58 (62, 66) B-sts; turn. With B-Side facing, using B, bind off loosely purlwise. Cut both yarns.

### FINISHING

Block lightly with steam. Graft shoulder sts, using Kitchener st and matching yarn, on each facing Side. Sew side seams. Graft closed the 2 Sides on hem at cast on rows and the bind off at neck. Pin collar, with cast on edge to neck edge, and main color facing, placing ¾" in from center Front on each side; graft Collar around neck edge on both Sides, using yarn to match the main color of each Side. Weave in ends.

# TECHNICAL TIPS

Some of the techniques I've presented in this book are novel, but the instructions have been written in standard knitting pattern language. Here are some tips to help you get the best results. On page 172 is a glossary of terms and abbreviations. All efforts have been made to ensure that the instructions are comprehensive and error-free. Please follow them carefully. Nevertheless, mistakes do happen—if you believe you've found one, please write to me by way of my publisher (Stewart, Tabori & Chang, 115 W. 18th St., New York, NY 10011) so I may address it.

## UNDERSTANDING SIZE/ MEASUREMENTS

The women's garments have been sized for the most part for Small, Medium, and Large. These sizes correspond to 31–34 (35–38, 39–42)" chest measured around the fullest part; in terms of average US manufacturer's dress sizes, they correspond to sizes 2–6 (6–10, 10–16). If your measurement falls between two sizes, make the smaller if you want body-conscious fit, make the larger if you want relaxed drape. If you are petite or plus size, you'll probably need to adjust the pattern so it is customized to your measurements; if you need help with this, ask at your local yarn shop or knitting guild.

Instructions are for smallest size with larger in parentheses. If there is another arrangement (i.e., < > for Child's sizes) it is stated in instructions. If one figure is given it applies to all sizes.

## GAUGE

Knitting to the tension given in the instructions is probably the most important factor in achieving good results. Get familiar with your own tendency to knit more tightly or loosely than suggested on the ball band. If you know you're usually tighter than average then try an 8 (5mm) needle instead of 7 (4.5mm) for worsted weight yarn, try 11 (8mm) instead of 10½ (6.5mm) for bulky, etc. To encourage you to swatch and match gauge, I have included 2 hats and a kerchief that also serve as gauge swatches for their projects. I urge you to extend this concept— make a practice of swatching and turn all your swatches into hats, bags, washcloths, pillows, etc.

## KEEPING TRACK OF ROWS/STS

Paying careful attention to RS and WS rows helps to keep in pattern and shape correctly. These are usually given in parentheses and you can also usually go by whether row number is odd or even. Unless otherwise stated, all EOR shaping is done on RS rows. When pattern states "end with WS row," the last row completed is WS (and vice versa).

Keeping track of stitch numbers helps to avoid mistakes. Whenever the stitch number changes, the new count is given following a long dash.

## READING SCHEMATICS

Reading information from schematics (the diagrams of sweater pieces) facilitates interpreting the pattern. They are shown as knit (not necessarily as worn) with the cast on edge toward bottom of page and bind off toward top. When Left Front or Sleeve is shown, it is the one that will be worn on the left side of the body (on right when RS facing). Measurement lines that curve with arrows at each end indicate circular knit.

## CASTING ON

Most of the patterns specify the long-tail cast-on method to obtain the results shown. If you favor another cast on (and like its outcome) then go right ahead. I prefer long-tail as it creates a firm but elastic edge from which it isn't easy to drop stitches accidentally on first round/row. It is actually equivalent to doing a single (backward loop) cast-on and then knitting 1 row, so the first row it presents shows the purl side. When doing the long-tail cast-on, be sure to allow a length of approx ½" (for thin yarn) to 1½" (for bulky) per stitch to be cast on as a "tail."

### BEGINNING TO WORK IN THE ROUND

Cast on number of stitches stated onto one of the tips of the circular needle. Spread the stitches across the circular needle from tip to tip. Fold the needle's cord to form a circle; the smooth edge of cast on should be facing out, and the bottom of stitches should be aligned, not twisted on the needle. The yarn will be extending from the RH needle to the back of work. Place marker (pm) on RH needle for beginning of round. Being careful not to twist stitches, join by knitting into first stitch on LH needle (this is the slip knot from the cast on). Continue to knit until you come to the marker (one round completed). Slip marker (sl m) and work another round, checking that stitches are still aligned at the lower edge and haven't somehow twisted over needle.

(Be sure to purchase the right length circular needle for the number of sts—needle should not be too long or the sts will get stretched out, and this will affect gauge and your knitting pleasure. Remember that you only require half the width of the piece as only half of each loop will be on each side of needle. If short circular needles feel awkward, try holding sts on one circular and knitting around with second, and switching off.)

### WORKING WITH DOUBLE-POINTED NEEDLES

Some sets of dpns contain 5 needles, but if there are not very many sts, 4 will suffice—a trio to hold sts in triangular round and a spare working needle. You will work across sts of first needle with the spare needle of set, then as that needle is freed up work across sts of next needle, etc., always creating a new spare as you work around.

### FIXING TWISTED CIRCULAR KNIT

If, within the first 3 or 4 rounds, you discover that you have got a twist, you can fix it rather than start over: Straighten and ease stitches over needle so that the only twist is located at last stitch of rnd. Drop that stitch down to first cast on loop—the ladder between the last and first sts of rnd will look like Jacob's Ladder rather than aligned rungs as it absorbs the twist—nevertheless, insert crochet hook into the loop from cast on row and latch up the sts as best you can.

### MIRRORED DECREASES

When opposing right-slanting and left-slanting decreases are paired they are called "mirrored," and you should strive for them to look equal but reversed. Some decreases twist the stitches and some do not. In order to make the directional decrease marks more pronounced, I like to use modified k2tog-tbl for the left-slanting dec in which the top (first) st is twisted but bottom is straight (whereas k2tog-tbl twists bottom as well). Work as foll: Sl next st from LH needle to RH needle purlwise; sl the 2nd st knitwise, to change its orientation; slip sts back to LH needle and k2tog-tbl.

To complete the pair, I like to use this right-slanting dec, which also twists the top (2nd) st, but not the bottom (1st) st. Work as foll: Sl next st from LH needle to RH needle purlwise; sl the 2nd st knitwise, to change its orientation; sl sts back to LH needle and k2tog.

### CENTERING INCREASES ABOVE DECREASES AND VICE-VERSA

This technique pertains to the Ballet T-Shirt and Yoke Vest. Increases done with k-f/b always create a new stitch

to the left of the original stitch, with a visible "bar" mark. In order to create the illusion of a central stitch with new stitches emanating from each side, a pair of stitches is used ("inc, inc") and it is the 2nd stitch that appears to be central. To decrease at each side of "center" with the same alignment, you will work to 1 stitch before the pair, dec, k1 (the 2nd st of pair), dec.

### SHORT ROW SHAPING

Wrap and turn (wrp-t) for short rows as follows:

With yarn held to front (purl position), slip next stitch from LH needle to RH needle purlwise (when you slip purlwise you do not change the orientation of the stitch on the needle); turn piece so WS is facing (the sts just worked, plus the slipped stitch, are now in the left hand); bring yarn to the front between the needles (purl position), return the slipped st to RH needle purlwise, <for St st, purl to end of row (knit the same stitches back to the other edge)> for Garter st or Rev St st, bring the yarn to the back between the needles (slipped stitch is wrapped and yarn is in the knit position, ready to work to end of row, which is where the Short Row began); knit to end of WS row, (knit the same stitches back to the other edge). Each subsequent pair of rows (one RS and one WS) make up one Short Row. For "top aligned" Short Rows, where all the wrapped stitches will end up at the top of the wedge, another stitch (or set of sts) will be left unworked as each Short Row is completed. For "bottom aligned" Short Rows, where all the wrapped stitches will end up at the bottom of the wedge, you will work more sts each time, working the wrap together with the stitch it surrounds as you pass it.

**approx** = approximately

**back loop** = the part of working st oriented in back of needle and to right

**beg** = begin; beginning

**bind off** = get rid of working sts and form a secure edge, at beg or middle of row/rnd, by working 2, then pass 1st over 2nd, work another, pass 2nd over 3rd, etc.

**CC** = contrast color

**cn** = cable needle

**cont** = continue; continuing

**dec** = decrease by working 2 (or more) sts together (note that "dec" usually counts as 2 sts in pattern row/rnd)

**EOR** = every other row

**each end** = at beg and end of row; at each edge of fabric

**est** = established

**dpn(s)** = double-pointed needle(s)

**foll** = follows; following

**front loop** = the part of working st oriented in front of needle and to left

**inc** = increase into next st usually by k-f/b (note that "inc" counts as 1 st in pattern row/rnd unless yo or m1 is specified)

**k** = knit

**k2tog** = knit 2 sts together (a right-slanting dec)

**k2tog-tbl** = knit 2 sts together through back loop (a left-slanting dec)

**k-f/b** = knit into front then back loop of same st to inc (aka "bar increase")

**Kitchener st** = a method of grafting rows of sts using tapestry needle and following path of a knit row much like duplicate st

**k-wise** = knitwise (as if to knit)

**LH** = left hand

**long-tail cast-on** = (aka Continental cast on) the most commonly used method

**mb** = make bobble as specified

**MC** = main color

**M1 or m1** = make 1—an inc done by lifting, twisting, and knitting into the strand between sts (aka "raised inc"); alternatively by not twisting strand can create eyelet inc

**p** = purl

**p2tog** = purl 2 sts together (a left-slanting dec, shows as right-slanting on reverse)

**p2tog-tbl** = purl 2 sts together through back loop (a right-slanting dec, shows as left-slanting on reverse)

**patt(s)** = pattern(s)

**p-f/b** = purl into front then back loop of same st to inc

**pm** = place marker

**psso** = pass the slipped stitch over

**p-wise** = purlwise (as if to purl)

**rem(s)** = remain(s); remaining

**rep** = repeat; repeating

**Rev St st** = reverse stockinette stitch

**RH** = right hand

**rnd(s)** = round(s)

**RS** = the right side of fabric (outward facing when worn)

**selvedge** = st(s) at an edge that are worked in a specified manner for neater appearance

**single cast-on** = (aka backward loop cast-on) form a simple loop on working yarn by folding inward and place it on needle

**skp** = slip 1, knit 1, psso (a left-slanting dec)

**sl** = slip

**sl m** = slip marker

**ssk** = slip, slip, knit (a left-slanting dec)

**st(s)** = stitch(es)

**shape; shaping** = an area in which you will dec and/or inc or otherwise change contours of piece

**Short Row(s)** = see page 171

**St st** = stockinette stitch (aka "jersey")

**tbl** = through back loop

**tog** = together

**work as for** = beg and follow instructions for other piece, with differences where specified

**work even** = cont without any shaping

**working sts** = (aka "live" sts) the sts on needle(s)

**wrp-t** = wrap and turn—see Short Rows, page 171

**WS** = the wrong side of fabric (inward facing when worn)

**wyib** = with yarn in back of the needle(s)

**wyif** = with yarn in front of the needle(s)

**yb** = place yarn to back between needle tips

**yf** = place yarn to front between needle tips

**yo** = yarn over—wrap yarn over RH needle from front to back; creates inc unless dropped on next row

**\*, \*\*** = single, double asterisk used as starting (and ending) point for pattern repeat

**( )** = parentheses used for instructions for alternate sizes, notes, or explanations

**< >** = angled brackets used for instructions for alternate sizes/styles

**[ ]** = brackets used for instructions to be worked as a group, notes, or explanations

To locate a retailer of the specific yarn used for the projects, contact the manufacturer/distributor listed below. All yarns and colors were available at time of publication. If the yarn becomes discontinued the company or a yarn shop can help you make a substitution based on the yarn weight, structure, and fiber content provided in the instructions. That information will also help you decide whether another yarn you're considering may work. Substitute yarns ideally should possess the same characteristics, but even with these may yield different results, so swatch to see if a desired effect is achieved. Be sure to purchase enough of a single dye lot to complete the project.

**Artful Yarns/JCA/Reynolds**
35 Scales La.
Townsend, MA 01469
978-597-8794

**Berroco**
14 Elmdale Rd., PO Box 367
Uxbridge, MA 01569
www.berroco.com

**Brown Sheep Company**
100662 County Rd. 16
Mitchell, NE 69357
800-826-9136
www.brownsheep.com

**Cascade Yarns**
1224 Andover Park East
Tukwila, WA 98188
800-548-1048
www.cascadeyarns.com

**Classic Elite**
300 Jackson St.
Lowell, MA 01852
800-444-5648
www.classiceliteyarns.com

**Crystal Palace Yarns—
Straw Into Gold, Inc.**
160 23rd St.
Richmond, CA 94804
www.straw.com

**Dale of Norway**
N16 W23390 Stoneridge Dr., Ste. A
Waukesha, WI 53188
262-544-1996
www.dale.no

**Goddess Yarns**
2911 Cavanaugh Blvd.
Little Rock, AR 72205
866-332-YARN
www.goddessyarns.com

**(Heirloom) Russi Sales Distribution**
605 Clark Rd.
Bellingham, WA 98225
360-647-8289
www.russisales.com

**Jaeger and Rowan**
Dist. by Westminster Fibers
4 Townsend West, Unit 8
Nashua, NH 03063
603-886-5041
wfibers@aol.com
www.knitrowan.com

**Joseph Galler, Inc.**
5 Mercury Ave.
Monroe, NY 10950
800-836-3314

**Karabella Yarns**
1201 Broadway
New York, NY 10001
800-550-0898
www.karabellayarns.com

**Lorna's Laces**
4229 North Honore St.
Chicago, IL 60613
773-935-3803
www.lornaslaces.net

**Muench**
1323 Scott St.
Petaluma, CA 94954
www.muenchyarns.com

**Mostly Merino**
P.O. Box 878
Putney, VT 05346
802-254-7436
merino@together.net

**Needful Yarns, Inc.**
4476 Chesswood Dr.
Toronto, ON M3J2B9
Canada
   OR
60 Industrial Pkwy. PMB #233
Cheektowaga, NY 14227
www.needfulyarnsinc.com

**Plymouth Yarn Co.**
500 Lafayette St.
PO Box 28
Bristol, PA 19007
215-788-0459
www.plymouthyarn.com

**Tahki-Stacy Charles, Inc.**
8000 Cooper Ave. Bldg 1
Glendale, NY 11385
800-338-YARN
www.tahkistacycharles.com

**Trendsetter Yarns**
6745 Saticoy St. #101
Van Nuys, CA 91406
818-780-5497

**NOTIONS**

**Active Trimming**
(zippers cut to size)
250 West 39th St.
New York, NY 10018
212-921-7114
www.activetrimming.com

**Greenberg & Hammer**
(buttons, buckles, toggles)
24 West 57th St.
New York, NY 10019
800-955-5135
www.greenberg-hammer.com

**M&J Trimming**
(carpetbag handle, lacings)
1008 Sixth Ave.
New York, NY 10018
800-9MJ-TRIM
www.mjtrim.com

# ACKNOWLEDGMENTS

DESIGNING, KNITTING, AND WRITING can be extremely solitary work. Each time I set out, it is like scaling a cliff to discover the limits of my capability; there are moments of fear and of exhilaration and in the end I need to know I have given my all during the creative process. This book project brought a personal challenge of a new magnitude and I realized early on that I couldn't accomplish it entirely on my own. Fortunately, a supportive network of colleagues, friends, family, students, customers, and knitting strangers came to my rescue during the yearlong trek. It is thanks to their help and support that the book got made.

I'm indebted to my editor, Melanie Falick, for recognizing my potential, helping to hone my vision, bringing out my best work, and for her friendship in stressful times. I hope we have created a book that is worthy of a place on the same shelf as her magnum opus of the knitting world, *Knitting In America*. I'm grateful for the expertise and hard work of graphic designer Anna Christian, copyeditor Betty Christiansen, and everyone else involved in getting the book to press. Photographer Adrian Buckmaster gave his talent and perspective, which captured the mood so brilliantly. And I appreciate all the people who made the photo shoots successful—Kristin Petliski for organizing and assisting me in styling, Angela Huff for makeup and awesome hair, Lisa Daehlin and Yelena Mironova for staying up all night with me sewing zippers and lining handbags before the final shoot. And, of course, thanks to the models, including the inimitable Jaime Coon, my beautiful sister Jessica Durham, my charming nieces Sophia and Haley Redding, my delightful daughter Olivia Garay Durham, and our wonderful friends from the Crosby Street playgroup, Tom and Oden Cote and Nattie and Lulu Johnson, and Rawn Harding, whom I discovered at the corner deli. Much of the book was photographed in New York's Central Park—one of my favorite spots on the planet—and at M'Finda Kalunga Community Garden on the Lower East Side.

Most important, I couldn't have presented this large collection without the knitters who put their energy into the sample garments. I usually like to make adjustments to my prototypes as I knit, so it was a new procedure to send my "babies" off to other hands. Thanks to the Upper West Side knitting group (Starbucks, 86th and Columbus, Wednesday nights) and the online Forum at www.knittersreview.com, I found local New York knitters as well as women across the country and in Canada who enthusiastically took on projects I wouldn't have had time to knit myself. They are Alexandra Halpin, Alison Green Will, Amanda Berka, Amy Backos, Anjeanette Milner, Carrie Brenner, Eileen Casey, Elaine Linet, Jeanine Bowen, Jennifer Johansmeyer, Jeri Jahns, Joan Dyer, Jodi Lewanda, Judi Anderson Seal, Judith Rothman, Juli Borst, Kathleen Catlett, Kristin Frazier, Lisa Daehlin, Lisa Farley, Louise Klaber, Monika Morovan, Naomi Dagen Bloom, Patricia Chen, Rebecca Hatcher, Susan Miles, Tacilya Grant, Tracey Dixon, Vanessa Wilmoth, and Vicki Sipkin. These knitters range from beginner to advanced and from twenty-something to eighty-something. Many told me they were in transition and participated as part of their personal quest; three were laid off from their jobs, three were moving house, and three got married during the year. And yet with these goings-on they persevered and their finished projects kept arriving, bolstering the progress of my own sample knitting. As we communicated sporadically over coffee and email, there were some serendipitous "misinterpretations" that allowed me to clarify and alter instructions or to decide to incorporate changes into the design for the better. I believe every knitter imbues her (or his) stitchwork with a quality as unique as her signature, and in this instance my crafty ladies have made their mark. I cannot thank them enough.

There are others who enabled me to get to this point in my career. I wouldn't be here without Trisha Malcolm, who gave me my first big break at *Vogue Knitting* and has continued to showcase my work over the years. I'm also grateful to Pam Allen and Ann Budd at *Interweave Knits* for their advice and support. Elyssa Meyrich of Sew Fast/Sew Easy mentored me on couture construction during midnight window shopping along Fifth Avenue. Diana Rupp at Make Workshop provided another ear to bend when I was overwhelmed. And Chuck Blackwell has always offered techie help, assembling my PC and creating my website. My students at The Open Center allowed me to learn how to teach knitting in my own manner. Thanks go to Aunt Alex and Mariann Nowack, fairy godmothers of sorts. Also the firms of Shea & Gould and Dewey Ballantine LLP let me take up my needles between documents as a knit-obsessed proofreader and so I was able to master the craft while holding a day job. And I appreciate all the strong women writers who have taught and encouraged me over the years—Susan Cheever, Sherrill Jaffe, Ann Snitow, Lynda Schorr, Jane Lazarre, Marguerite Young. Little did I know it would be a knitting book in which I would put it to use. And, lastly, thanks to Milton Garay for making me the mother of a wonderful child and fueling my ambition.